D0297589

Two Goldies in repose

Hearts, Minds and Paws

A book on dogs and working dogs

Nina Bondarenko

Aeneas Press
&
Canine Partners

First published in 2007
by Aeneas Press

PO Box 200
Chichester
West Sussex
PO18 0YX
UK

Designed and typeset
by Marie Doherty

Printed and bound in Croatia

ISBN: 1-902115-62-7

British Library Cataloguing in Publication Data
A catalogue record of this book is available from the British Library

Bondarenko, Nina

About the Author

Nina Bondarenko is the Director of Canine Training Development for the UK national charity Canine Partners which provides highly-trained dogs to help people with disabilities. Starting life in Australia, Nina has travelled all over the world, learning about dogs and teaching others – from Police Dog Handlers to pet owners. She has judged internationally, demonstrated for HM The Queen, developed the 'Puppy Education System® of errorless learning' and for 15 years has helped build and develop the Canine Partners charity, a member of Assistance Dogs International and a leader in the Assistance Dog field. She is an internationally renowned lecturer, educator and trainer of dogs. A consultant for the International Association of Animal Behaviour Counsellors, Nina is also the presenter of the training video: 'Understanding and Training your Puppy'. Her advice is sought all over the world.

Nina with German Shepherd Dog and Rottweiler puppies

Chairman David Newberry and Yargo

Anne Conway (left), one of three Founders, with human puppy!

Contents

Foreword

by His Royal Highness The Duke of Gloucester KG GCVO, Patron of Canine Partners

Those of us who are used to the idea of having dogs as pets, and the role they play as a member of the family, will have observed that there is a huge variation in the characters of individual dogs and in their varied ways of expressing themselves. The pleasure that a dog can take in his environment and exploring it to the maximum, is easy to share and enjoy with the human master.

Canine Partners has demonstrated that the 'responsibility' that a dog owner takes in looking after his 'pet' is not necessarily a one-way affair, but that given the right training, a dog too can take responsibility for his charge, particularly if they have a handicap – and become a team member in overcoming life's major problems.

This book takes a careful look at all the attributes and capabilities that dogs can develop, if needed, and how they can transform the lives of those with whom they form partnerships, in so many different ways.

I hope the readers of this book will enjoy the stories portrayed and appreciate that here is a resource with immense potential for development; and that further support for Canine Partners will demonstrate more possibilities for human canine teamwork, that will prove of huge significance to those whose needs are still to be resolved.

Richard, Duke of Gloucester
October 2006

Her Majesty The Queen talks to Gareth Flather OBE and Gracie. Gary is a highly regarded member of the Judiciary and Gracie attends all his Court hearings! In 2004, Her Majesty honoured the Charity, by summoning a team to Windsor Castle, for a private demonstration of the dogs' skills.

Acknowledgements

The idea for this book was cooked up, almost literally, over dinner one night, between the Publisher and Chief Executive of the Charity, Canine Partners. The Charity's Programme Director, Nina Bondarenko, with all her background, expertise and knowledge was the perfect author for it and began work immediately, about one year ago. It has been a fascinating path to tread and one that hopefully you will enjoy too.

While the stories and experiences include work from all over the world, the majority of it centres around the United Kingdom and especially the amazing world of the assistant dogs: Canine Partners, Hearing Dogs and Guide Dogs in particular.

We would like to acknowledge contributions to the work from so many people, it is difficult to know where to start: to Anand Kumar, who gave that dinner party, to the Trustees, staff and volunteers of Canine Partners who all made it possible, to the Partners of our dogs – those wonderful people who sometimes against all odds, bounce back more determined than ever, to overcome insuperable difficulties and still come up smiling; and of course to the dogs themselves: happy, willing, amazingly clever, cuddly, funny, heart-rendingly loyal and hard working, in their unspoken and unswerving mission to assist mankind. We gratefully acknowledge the help provided by Neil Ewart for his contribution of Chapter 6 and to Caroline Scott whose article on Frodo first appeared in the Sunday Times Magazine in 2000.

We would also like to thank the myriad people, companies, trusts and foundations, both large and small, who have at one time or another, over the past 14 years, contributed to the ever-burgeoning success of Canine Partners. In particular, invidious though it might be to single a few out of so many, the enormous support given to us by our sponsors, including Nestlé Purina, Zurich Financial Services, Morgan Stanley Investment, the Henry Smith Trust, MWE, Alan Jukes OBE (who personally gave so much more than the widow's mite), The Kennel Club, our bankers Lloyds TSB, The Big Lottery and all those wonderful community-based organisations, such as Rotary, Soroptimists, Lions, Round Table, the Masons, and on and on … through ten thousand individuals – you know who you are!

We have also been blessed by a number of well-known people who have supported us and made this story possible, including Helena Bonham-Carter and all her family, Jenny Seagrove, Shauna Lowry, Rolf Harris, Graham Norton and other stars – and a host of well-known public and household names, who would be embarrassed if we mentioned them, but who give unstinting effort and support, to raise funds for the ongoing work of the Charity in training dogs to assist people with disabilities. Thank you all for unselfishly giving of your time.

Of course we acknowledge our Founders, three extraordinary ladies: Anne Conway, Nicky Pendleton and Liz Ormerod, who set up the Charity in the early 1990s. On her part, Nina would like to thank a raft of friends and colleagues including Karen Pryor, Bob Bailey, Gary Wilkes, Gwen Bailey, Roger Mugford, Neil Ewart and Sarah Fisher.

Finally in acknowledging too the splendid support of our Vice Patrons, the Countess of Clarendon DL, Lord Kindersley, Roger Jefcoate CBE and our Vice Presidents, this book is respectfully dedicated to our Patron, His Royal Highness the Duke of Gloucester KG GCVO.

Terry Knott, CEO Canine Partners
October 2006

Introduction

by Rosemary Smart,
Chief Executive of The Kennel Club

I was delighted to be asked by Canine Partners (CP) to write the Introduction to this book and indeed feel honoured to do so.

The Kennel Club has enjoyed a close affiliation with Canine Partners over many years since its inception 16 years ago and the work that the Charity and these amazing dogs do on behalf of their human partners on a daily basis and the promotion of dogs in general to a wider audience, is truly inspirational.

We all know that dogs are amazing creatures and are our ultimate companions, having evolved with man over thousands of years. Assistance dogs really are the cream of the crop, bringing to their partners independence, self worth, a sense of being, interest and sociability and in so many instances these special dogs have quite literally saved people's lives by giving them a reason to live again.

On behalf of the Kennel Club, I have personally attended a number of receptions, open days and functions hosted by Canine Partners – and the organisation regularly attends *Crufts* and *Discover Dogs* in London. When you learn first hand of the remarkable and heart warming stories that benefactors share with you, it really does reaffirm to me, each time, just how adaptable and versatile 'man's best friend' really is and how remarkable these dogs are.

They demonstrate patience, intelligence, kindness and eagerness in their willingness to please – all in equal measure – and really are central to turning people's lives around for the better.

CP, as an organisation, is very close to the Kennel Club's heart and has received funding over the years from our Charitable Trust to assist with the excellent work that they do. This work is superb and they are to be applauded for it, bringing together dogs and man in the ultimate caring partnership. The charity was accredited as a centre of excellence by Assistance Dogs International in 2006 and I still cannot believe that they are only 16 years young, especially when I think of all they have achieved to date. I think that they will be the first to admit that there is still much work to do and long may this continue.

This book bears testament to Canine Partners as an organisation – to its management and staff for their tireless efforts, carers, donors, volunteers and, of course, the dogs. The charity really does provide the ultimate partnership between man, woman and dog and opens the doors wide to independence.

I'm sure that you will enjoy this book as much as I did, as it is informative, fun, humorous, at times sad, and throughout – enthralling. It deserves to grace every table and shelf throughout the land – and beyond!

With most of the proceeds and profits being handed back to Canine Partners, purchasers can rest assured that their money is being particularly well spent and reinvested in the Charity, to enable it to continue its extremely worthwhile and hugely important work.

So please do read, enjoy and marvel at these amazing dogs and partnerships which really do 'enhance the quality of life and open doors to independence', not to mention all the other amazing dogs mentioned in this book.

Rosemary Smart with her dog Rufus

Preface

Concepts: the Book and the Charity

This book is about dogs and the extraordinary role that they can play in our lives. A vast number of people have dogs and an even bigger number come into contact with them, every day of their lives. Love them or hate them, they are here to stay!

When it comes down to it, humans and dogs are both species of animals: the one allegedly more advanced than the other. Yet as we so clearly show here, dogs actually have the edge on us in many different ways. Their hearing, smell and in some ways their sight, is vastly better than ours and they have other abilities that perhaps atrophied in mankind thousands of years ago. For example how do dogs know when an earthquake is coming, days before it happens? How do dogs tell that an epileptic fit is about to occur? Mankind cannot afford to feel smug about the supremacy issue and we should perhaps acknowledge that in partnership together we are very often stronger than the actual sum of the two parts.

The reason a dog has so many friends is that he wags his tail instead of his tongue.

—Anonymous

Hearts Minds and Paws covers all the myriad aspects of the canine world, as it impinges on and enhances our lives: humour, love, sorrow, pathos, academic and instructional, plus a welter of illustrations by Nina herself and many lovely, quirky, amusing photographs, from all over the world – there is something here for everyone.

Canine Partners – A Centre of Excellence

Originally founded in 1990, through the energetic campaigning of Dr Elizabeth Ormerod MRCVS, Mrs Anne Conway and Mrs Nicky Pendleton SROT, Canine Partners has steadily developed from a wonderful idea, to an established, nationally-based charity, with its own purpose-built Training Centre, opened in 2005. This extraordinary success story is based on the endless generosity of not only the great British public and British business, in terms of donating money and equipment to support the growth and development of the Charity, but also on the tireless efforts of the trainers, other staff and volunteers (including gallant Trustees), who are responsible for creating the spirit and the reality of this organisation.

So many people, especially during the ground-breaking early years, gave freely of their time on nights, weekends and public holidays, to ensure that this idea – to train selected dogs to a very high standard, so that they could assist people living with disability, in their daily lives – would become reality. The guiding principle of this work has been that the dogs would be trained and developed through the most modern and innovative training approaches, with the basis of the relationship with the person being mutual co-operation, respect and love.

Canine Partners has now become associated with award-winning dogs that are able to work above and beyond the original training, to truly assist their individual Partners to enjoy enhanced quality of life and independence. The Charity was accredited as a centre of excellence by Assistance Dogs International in 2006.

Terry Knott, CEO of Canine Partners, sees the future of Canine Partners as a truly national organisation, with Puppy Training Satellites throughout the United Kingdom and Ireland, backed up by the main Training Centre, London SW, and another subsidiary Training Centre in Scotland. He says: 'The incidence of general disabilities is increasing in the UK and depending upon which organisations in government and elsewhere that you talk to, there are some 8.5 to 10.5 million people registered disabled in the UK! Following our own detailed study, using figures supplied by the various disability agencies, at the very

Left: No, I'm not winking at girls – it's something in my eye!

least this indicates a role and need for assistance dogs for some 65,000 to 80,000 clients, which figure dwarfs the total production of assistance dogs (including Guide Dogs) in the UK, by a factor of ten.'

Training requirements

Assistance dogs need to be extensively socialised from a very early age, to a wide range of situations, sounds, and experiences. The dogs are also required to learn self-control over their natural canine inclinations, to greet and socialise with other dogs, to return greetings from people calmly, and to overcome any inherent predatory behaviour. Additionally Canine Partners' puppies need to learn component behaviours and problem solving.

Training approach

For the specialist, Canine Partners use the 'Puppy Education System®'; Inductive Retrieve; 'Operant Conditioning' with special emphasis on Homing Signals; errorless learning and the *Premack Principle*. Motivationally-based learning utilising play, food and touch, as well as life rewards and other motivators, is the basis for the puppy's education, which begins at the age of 7–8 weeks.

Range of tasks possible

These include walking beside a wheelchair or scooter, pressing a switch, unzipping a jacket, opening and loading or unloading a washing machine; retrieve named items to hand, lap, basket, counter, or other person; taking off jacket, trousers, skirt, scarf or other items of clothing, stabilising a person when walking or transferring; assisting a person to transition from floor to wheelchair, or chair or standing position; selecting items from shelves, or cupboards; holding a heavy door open; closing house or cupboard doors; opening sliding or hinged doors; pushing paralysed limbs back into place (arms, head, legs or feet); fetching human assistance; pressing emergency alarm phone; rolling person into recovery position; covering person with blanket; helping take off or put on bed covers such as duvets; interrupting unwanted or repetitious behaviour such as occurs during Parkinson's disease, anxiety attacks, or self-mutilation; maintaining contact with a person whilst that person is in distress or danger; responding in emergency or during any episodes or seizures; indicating oncoming medical situation such as low blood pressure, migraines, or epileptic seizures.

In summary, the scope to develop the concept of Canine Partners and similar dogs is immense. Achievements over the past 15 years of this comparatively young charity show the enormous potential to transform lives and open doors to independence, for people with major disabilities, both in practical and mechanical terms, but also in the love and therapeutic benefit a dog can give a human; and vice versa!

These skills are all very well, you might say, but of course they teach us to appreciate what most dogs, if properly trained, can do to make our lives easier, richer and better, as working dogs or simply as companions.

Whether you want the Rolls Royce or the Mini model of dog, time spent dipping into this book will hopefully be a happy, fulfilling and instructive experience and perhaps leave you with some great ideas and a fuller appreciation of the ways that dogs can enrich all our lives.

24
2006

Chapter ONE

The Human–Animal Bond

This book is about dogs and particularly working dogs. We know that in the hierarchy of domesticated animals, dogs in all manners of breeds, sizes, colours and capabilities have a central role in our lives. In the majority of cases the relationship is one as a friend, pet, family member and more. As Milan Kundera the Czech writer observed, "*The dog is our link to paradise. He knows not evil or jealousy or discontent. To sit with a dog on a hillside on a glorious afternoon is to be back in Eden, where doing nothing was not boring – it was peace.*"

'We give dogs time we can spare, space we can spare and love we can spare. And in return, dogs give us their all. It's the best deal man has ever made.'

—M. Acklam

In almost all instances the dog, whether as a friend, pet, family member, or for that matter a working companion, is skilful, perceptive and highly intelligent in the ever-increasing and diverse roles that they perform in our everyday lives and work.

It is also true that we almost take it for granted that dogs can learn to work in a thoughtful, nurturing and pro-active way with a person – with their hearts, minds and paws.

No matter how many dogs I train and place, I still wonder at the capacity of a dog to communicate and interact in such a profoundly insightful way. And yet they are all very matter-of-fact about it. There's no drama – they just get on with it!

When I was asked to set up a programme for Canine Partners to train dogs to assist people with disability in 1992, I already had an inkling of how dogs could work co-operatively with people. I was filming with my dog, a male Rottweiler named Yossarian, for a TV show in Melbourne, Australia. This dog worked as a Security Dog at weekends, and competed in Schutzhund trials, so he was well used to taking on armed suspects, or stopping the attack of an assailant. But on this day, he was required to stay absolutely still for 3 minutes in the dark and stare at a fixed point (this was before digital animation) as the cameras rolled. Unfortunately, we were filming the series in the Australian bush in summer during the day – there were no dark places. So the only place for the filming that they could find, was a huge clump of blackberry bushes, growing down the sides of a ravine.

This powerful dog had to hang down inside the bushes, clinging by his toes, scratched and cut by the thorns, and stay perfectly still, whilst watching my upheld finger. The fact that he did this perfectly, without complaint, for a young, inexperienced woman trainer, for nothing more than a squeeze, a scratch on the back and a game of tuggy, taught me first-hand the remarkable capacity to be helpful that some dogs can demonstrate, if they trust the owner and the owner respects the dog.

Puppies come into the training programme full of giggles and wiggles, and the joy is that they retain this delight in life, throughout a working career. The training process that I later developed for Canine Partners (then Assistance Dogs for Disabled People), allowed

And you'll never guess what she said my dear …

the dogs to teach me far more about how dogs think and learn and feel, than any course I had been on. Canine Partners training is based on teaching dogs to problem-solve, based upon my experience that dogs can learn vocabulary, sentences, context, and intent, and they can make informed decisions in a given or unfamiliar situation that benefit directly or indirectly the human partner. Having a mind that can plan, associate, rehearse and also empathise with another species is necessary, most especially for assistance dogs but for all other operational dogs.

For Canine Partners, having the capacity and desire to problem-solve and to come up with helpful behaviours in unfamiliar situations, is an essential for an effective working relationship with the disabled human partner. The fact that it is coupled with a sense of fun and mischief is part of the magic, and is due to the positive training methods used.

The idea that a dog has thought, insight and intention can be a difficult one for many people to accept. And yet, if dogs didn't have these qualities, there would have been none of the strong human–animal bond experiences that all of us who have dogs have enjoyed, none of the many stories in this book, stories of dogs like Endal or Orca who went on to win medals for Devotion to Duty. And if they hadn't possessed those qualities, they wouldn't have had a sense of humour – and any dog owner knows that dogs certainly have one of those! It is great to have a dog that can think for itself, but dogs love amusing themselves and their owners, by being unexpected, a little bit naughty, or even just frivolous! Yet when it is really important, a trained dog can truly rise above human expectations.

Give a dog a bone

Picture the scene: Gibson the young Golden Retriever was lying outside the house in the sun chewing a bone. Inside, his partner Roy was working at his specially adapted computer. They have been partnered for six months. Roy's condition required him to have instant communication with his working wife in a medical emergency, but suddenly the phone dropped onto the carpet. Roy sat there, unhappy about the thought of

disturbing his dog – who was relaxing in the garden, but anxious about not having the phone to hand. Suddenly the dog appeared with the bone in his mouth. Gibson placed the bone on Roy's lap, picked up the phone and handed it to Roy, then carefully took back his bone and returned to the garden. All without a word being spoken by Roy, who was too dumbfounded to speak! But not too dumbfounded to call me immediately to tell me what had happened!

Why would a dog do that? What would motivate a dog to interrupt his own pleasure to do something for a new owner, without command, or coercion, or indeed the offer or expectation of a reward? I hope this book goes some way towards explaining how we can interact with and work together with dogs so that they are able to give back to us their unique gifts. We have so many stories at Canine Partners, testifying to the unique relationship that is possible between a working dog and its owner or handler. The handler may be a complete novice dog owner, or may be restricted in mobility of hands, arms, fingers, face and body. Yet the dog continues to offer appropriate and helpful responses throughout a working life that may last up to 13 years. And do it with a wag of the tail, a big doggy grin and a wink.

Handlers and trainers of the other working dogs featured in this book also testify to the spirit of cooperation and 'work ethic' that the dogs show. People may say 'all dogs want to please'; others will claim that the dog is only doing the equivalent of 'hunting for its dinner', or that the dog is behaving like a robot and only doing what has been 'programmed'.

So how is it possible for the dogs in this book to offer their hearts, minds and paws willingly, freely and reliably, in cooperative partnership with people, who reward with praise, games, food, free play in the woods, swims in the sea and splashes in mud puddles? The trainers in this book consider it an absolute priority to ensure that the dog be motivated and enjoy working. The handlers enjoy being with their dogs, and form a close bond and rapport that can develop over time almost into a 'mind meld', where dog and person think as a team instead of as individuals. Yes, I have had dogs arrive at my house with difficult, dangerous, and entrenched behaviour problems. But I have never needed anything more than a knowledge of dog behaviour and cognition, the capacity to work out what is uniquely rewarding to that dog, and the confidence to set boundaries and stick to them without anger, or threats.

In this book, we hope to give you a sense of the extraordinary abilities and capacities of dogs, as revealed in their working relationships with people. By using rewards and encouragement, dogs are now demonstrating how profoundly they understand the human world and how prepared they are to co-operate, from their hearts and paws, to help people lead a more rewarding life. Dogs may have amazing senses of smell, of observation, and of hearing, but this is meaningless if they are not prepared to share these abilities and work alongside people to achieve a common goal.

We will talk about some of the special dogs that have either developed a skill due to their qualities of character or attitude, brought out by creative training, or were able to demonstrate abilities above and beyond their training, due to their unique relationship with the owner. We will also offer pain-free hints on assessing and selecting the puppy that's right for you, and be on hand with helpful advice as your puppy is

Not the dead fish! Puppies love to eat smelly things

Above: Miriam & Kruger

Opposite page
Top right: Kate & Lotoya
Bottom left: Dee & Sigbi
Bottom right: Nina & Hugo

wobbling through babyhood, bouncing and biting into kindergarten, leaping into teenage tantrums, and suddenly growing a brain and becoming your favourite family member – co-operative, fun and socially flexible. Who knows what extraordinary feats your new puppy will achieve, if life is begun in the most positive way?

The relationship between a dog and owner and working dog and handler or partner relies upon co-operation and mutual trust. This book is about the ways in which people give their hearts to dogs, and the ways in which dogs use their minds, hearts and paws to reciprocate.

When we started the training programme at Canine Partners, I thought I knew all about what dogs could do for people. I had been training dogs for over 30 years, for a very wide range of tasks, including assisting people with disability. However it was only when I started teaching the dogs the special skills they would need, to assist the people who were applying for a Canine Partners assistance dog, that I really started to learn what dogs could do.

Many times the dogs would teach me, because they would offer a solution to a perplexing problem, or they would suggest new skills that I could teach the others. Examples of this occurred very early on in training the first group of dogs. One young Golden Retriever, named Alex, was learning how to carry out a long sentence of requests. 'Go into the kitchen, up table, get the book, bring it here and put it in the basket.' He went off dutifully, got the book off the counter, and brought it to me. He dropped it into the basket, but it was a long, narrow book, and it landed sideways on the rim of the basket. I looked at it, laughed, and said 'Oh well, technically it is in the basket!'

Alex looked at me, looked at the book, wagged his tail slowly, and then reached up a paw, and tipped the book into the basket. He then looked at me with a big grin on his face, wagging furiously. I blinked, and then cheered him, clapped him and hugged him for being such a big-brained fellow. Later on, when he was placed with 6'6" Ian Free, he had to work out how to put the keys exactly into Ian's bent fingers – due to a

high level spinal injury, caused by a diving accident. Ian couldn't open or close his fingers – so that they didn't drop. No problem for the clever little dog!

Another from that first 'A' team of Golden Retrievers was Alfred. He had been placed with Allen Parkin, whose Multiple Sclerosis was suddenly deteriorating, which meant he could not feel the objects that the dog was handing him. This meant that he frequently dropped them, but Alfred just picked them up and tried to give them to him again. When this became too difficult, Allen was deeply distressed because he thought that the dog would be taken back to Canine Partners. However Alfred had other ideas.

He observed Allen intently, then thoughtfully and carefully, picked up the purse, stood on Allen's knees and pushed the purse into Allen's mouth! Allen was in tears of laughter but also relief because, by holding onto the object with his teeth, he could feel it sufficiently to be able to take hold of it correctly. When he rang me to tell me, I suddenly realised that, if the dog hadn't shown me what he could do to solve the problem, I probably would have taken the dog back. For the dog to recognise that the man's mouth is the same as the long, pointy and black-nosed muzzle of a dog, is extraordinary, and for the dog to make the effort to help his handler to that extent, indicates just how much some dogs understand about their role and the way that they can interact with humans.

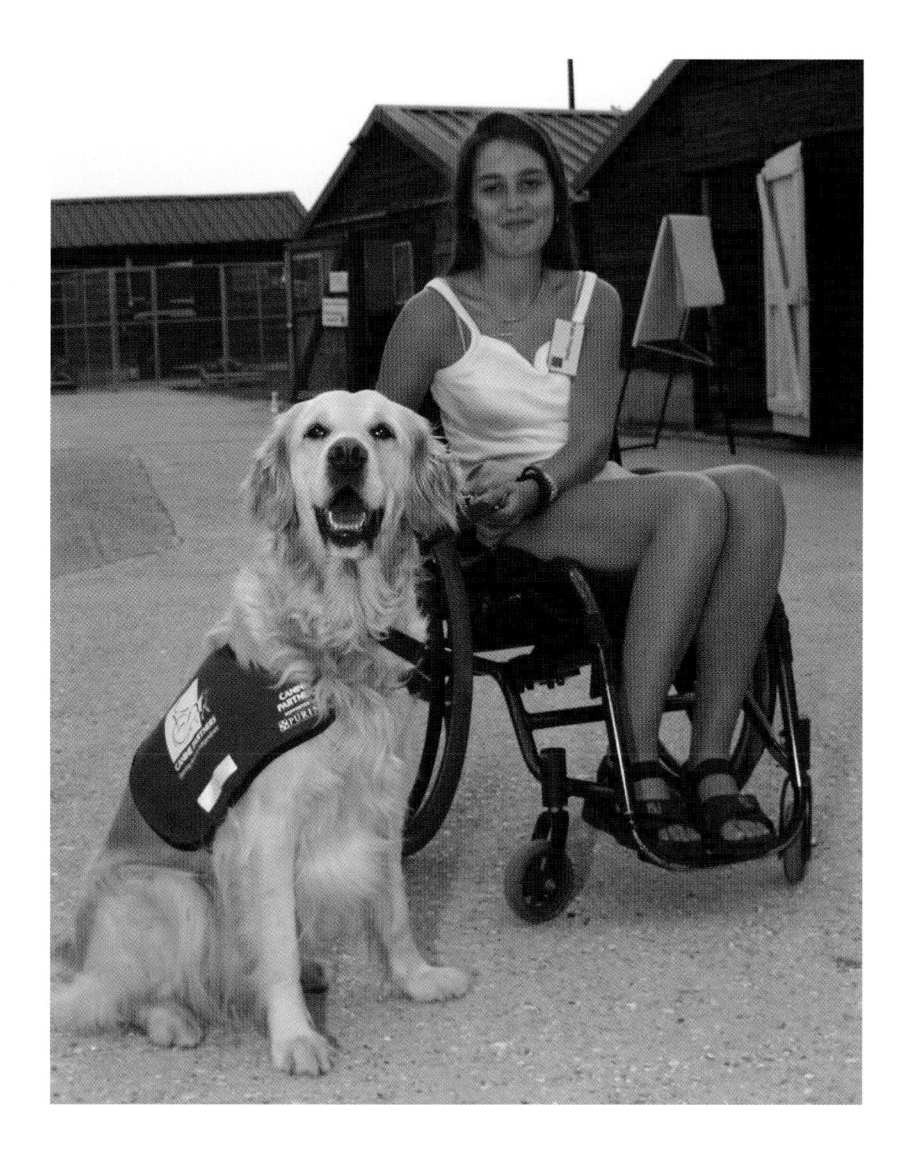

2005

Chapter TWO

Canine Super-Heroes

The following stories are about two very special dogs, trained by Canine Partners and acknowledged for their achievements with the highest award a dog can receive – The peacetime PDSA Medal for Devotion to Duty. This is the canine equivalent to the George Cross and it is testimony to these wonderful dogs, their dedicated handlers and the motivational training that they received, that both dogs were recognised in this way

'If there are no dogs in Heaven, then when I die I want to go where they went.'
—Will Rogers

Have you ever questioned and wondered what really happens to all those injured war heroes that return from the world's conflicts? No fanfare or banner-waving crowds greets their arrival home. Cosseted away in near secrecy, an RAF medical evacuation plane touches down at some obscure military airport. A quick transfer to the back of awaiting ambulances and those that have made the penultimate sacrifice for the defence of the realm come home. Most of these injured personnel become no more than newspaper statistics – today's news, yet tomorrow's fish and chip paper. They melt quietly into obscurity and continue fighting an everyday battle of survival in an attempt to eke a very basic standard of living on a modest war pension. Often these injured heroes find themselves thrown on the mercy and kindness of the many others, reliant on the many service charities. Most, though, are far too proud to ask for help and valiantly struggle on.

For one such war hero, who suffered major injuries in the 1991 Gulf War which left him with severe physical and mental trauma, help came from a totally unexpected quarter and has transformed his life and that of his family.

CANINE PARTNER ENDAL

'I was in the darkest place when I returned from the Gulf War, hospitalised and with no future and no past that I could remember. Endal lifted me into the light and he has taught me that angels have four legs and a wet nose!' (Allen Parton)

The Japanese television crew watched, cameras whirling, as Endal, the yellow Labrador leaped up at the cash machine and then, with his mouth, 'handed' the credit card and a wad of £10 notes to his master, 42-year-old Allen Parton. 'That's amazing,' said producer Masaki Mochizuki from Super Television, one of Japan's national television networks. 'What else can he do?'

Endal was keen to show him. Back at Allen's home in Clanfield, Hampshire, he opened the washing machine with his nose, pulled out several pairs of socks, carefully dropping them into the laundry basket ready to hang on the line. Then, on command, he opened a kitchen cupboard, tugging at a purple cord hanging from the handle, and nosed out a packet of cereal, carrying it in his mouth to Allen in his wheelchair. Finally, he sat on the chair at the kitchen table,

Honestly, these Chip and Pins are the limit!

while Allen had breakfast, ready to 'hand' him anything if he needed it.

Four years earlier, however, when Endal was born, no one thought that this lonely little puppy was particularly special. Nina's instinct, which she has learned to rely on during her 30 years experience, told her that even if Endal wasn't as keen as she hoped, he would be right one day for someone.

So Nina bought him from the breeder Barry Edwards, and placed him with Puppy Parent volunteer Judith Turner, and he continued through a lively puppyhood on into advanced training. Yet as Endal continued training with a half-hearted attitude at the Training Centre, Nina couldn't help thinking there was something missing. Somehow, despite his obvious intelligence, the dog lacked dynamism and didn't seem to sparkle. It was as though he was waiting for something or someone to happen in life, in order to release his inner energy. Endal was also the kind of puppy who was choosy about who he bonded with. When, as part of his training, he did a 3-week swap with another family to help him adapt to different environments, Endal took a while to adjust. Although he did what he was told, he could also close down and withdraw into himself. Nina began to realise that she needed to find him a full-time partner whom he could really relate to. If she couldn't find the right person, Endal would never reveal his full potential.

There was also another added complication. Endal was showing signs of going lame. 'Puppies often do this, on and off, as part of their growing process while their bones knit together,' explained Nina. 'It's known as panosteitis, like growing pains in children. But it was happening too often to Endal so we had him x-rayed. The results showed that he might have osteochondritis dessicans (OCD), a fault in the elbow joint. Some dogs get better on their own accord, but others get worse and have to be operated on, which would mean they wouldn't be able to work. We weren't sure with Endal. He seemed too good a dog to waste but at the same time, his future was seriously in doubt. So we decided to rest him and see what happened.'

Meanwhile, only five miles away, the future was looking even bleaker for 42-year old Allen Parton. In 1991, Allen, then a weapons electronics officer in the Royal Navy, had waved goodbye to his wife Sandra and their two children, Liam and Zoe, age 6 and 5, to fight in the Gulf War. As they set off, Allen and his men had been told that 15 per cent of them wouldn't be coming back, but like many brave servicemen, Allen was certain this wouldn't apply to him. After all, he'd already served in the Falklands and Northern Ireland and come out unscathed. Why should his luck run out this time?

It did run out. Within a month of arriving, Allen's military car was smashed up in a serious accident,

What is Osteochondrosis?

OCD is a bone disease in which normal cartilage development fails. It is usually seen in puppies, often in the elbow and shoulder joints. It can lead to osteoarthritis as the dog ages and is most common in large and giant breeds.

The condition may cause lameness on the affected leg and the dog may have abnormal posture or gait. Treatment can involve surgery, painkillers and anti-inflammatories. The dog's weight and exercise should be controlled to keep the condition stable.

Canine Partner Endal close up

which shattered both his body and mind for ever. His first memory was waking up in a British hospital 6 weeks later and thinking, 'Where am I?' His right-hand side had lost all feeling and he had lost 50 per cent of his memory. The effects were catastrophic: Allen couldn't recognise family or friends, let alone remember the names for simple items like 'bed'. He only knew Sandra was his wife because the nurses would say: 'Your wife is here'. Even more terrifying, he couldn't recall getting married or having the children. In a flash – literally – Allen had gone from a healthy father of two children to an angry, wheelchair-bound invalid who couldn't talk properly and whose words spilled out of his mouth in a haphazard, disorderly fashion without making sense.

'The fear and shock made me furious,' admits Allen. 'I refused to accept I was disabled and I'm ashamed to say that I was horrible and rude to everyone.' He was also plunged into a deep, fathomless depression from which there seemed no escape. Twice, he tried to commit suicide. It was, he told himself, the only way out.

Opposite page
Top: Endal helps Allen get his jacket off
Bottom: Endal picks Allen's favourite cereal

Allen spent the next 5 years in hospital and rehabilitation. When he finally came home, Sandra, who had had to give up her job as a nurse to look after her husband, was at her wits' end. Then she saw an article about the Charity Canine Partners in a local newspaper. Desperate to do something for herself, as well as looking after Allen, she became a puppy walker to Ferdy, a yellow Labrador. The distraction and light-relief provided by a lively puppy in the house, helped the whole family – even though Allen still found it difficult to talk and communicate.

One day, in the summer of 1997, Allen's usual bus for his day-centre failed to turn up. Sandra told him, in no uncertain terms, that she wasn't prepared to have him moping around the house. He would have to go to the Canine Partners training centre with her. Although they didn't see it then, fate had just stepped in. Allen's life was about to change in almost as dramatic a way as his accident. As he sat in the training centre that morning, in his wheelchair parked in the corner of the room, refusing to speak or join in, Allen didn't realise this. Instead, he would rebuff anyone who tried to ask him a question by telling them to talk to his wife. He felt horribly self-conscious and it was easy to see why. Not only was he unable to speak clearly, but his body was continually twitching. He refused to make eye contact with anyone and was very self-conscious and uncomfortable.

Allen & Endal – my partner and I

Not far away from his chair sat a group of puppies, resting in between training sessions. One of them was Endal. 'He started looking at Allen and as he did so, Allen glanced back,' said Nina, who is constantly observing dogs and thinking about the applicants, to see if they might fit. Endal then looked up again and seemed to say, 'Mmm, I quite like you', and then Allen put his hand down to give him a pat. Immediately, Endal leaped up on Allen's lap and gave a big slobbery grin. Allen smiled as though to say 'This dog really likes me!' Then, almost without knowing why he was doing it, Allen began to rub Endal under his jacket. It so happened that Endal LOVES being rubbed at exactly that spot. He looked up at Allen as if to say: 'You are my man!'

'It was nothing short of a miracle; a dramatic turning point, which both Allen and Endal had needed so badly in their lives and it sent,' says Nina, a tingle down her spine. As Allen left the centre that day, there was a certain sparkle in his eyes, which hadn't been there for a very long time. As Nina points out, until he met Allen, Endal hadn't been anything special. It was the combination of his character with Allen's that made the winning ticket: two parts really are greater than the whole.

The decision to apply for a dog took Allen just moments to make – then came the assessment procedures and paperwork to go through. 'I had to fill in a form, describing my disabilities and this was the first time I had admitted there was something wrong with me,' recalls Allen. 'It was a cathartic experience, which finally gave me the hope I needed. Until I met him, I was in the depths of despair, but when he refused to leave my side in that training centre, I suddenly saw a chink of light. Endal had found me and wasn't going to let me go. He was living proof that *angels* don't just come on two legs.' Nina also commented: 'He seemed to understand how much Allen had been through. Endal's an interesting combination of pushiness and sensitivity.'

Endal's most valuable skill is his ability to use his initiative and quickly read situations. This was exactly what Allen needed to help him cope with his severe injuries. Would Endal be able to help? They would soon find out when he joined the Parton household full-time in autumn, 1997. Still unable to speak properly, Allen also suffered from word blindness when he simply couldn't find the words to give Endal a command. 'One morning, I realised I'd left my electric razor upstairs. I could see a picture of the razor in my head, but couldn't think of its name. I was rubbing my beard, trying to think of the magic word when, to my amazement, he ran up the stairs and came down with it in its leather case.'

Over the ensuing months, Allen and Endal began to create their own sign language. A pat on the head means that Allen wants his cap. Instantly, Endal darts round to the back of the wheelchair where the cap is inside Allen's bag. Hands held up mean gloves are required and Endal finds them and brings them round the front to Allen.

Allen and Endal began to be photographed by local newspapers and then, as they grew in confidence, they were nominated for an award in a national competition run by *Dogs Today* magazine. During one photographic session, Endal and Allen went shopping at the local supermarket to show how Endal could differentiate between 'tins' and 'bottles' and nose out whatever Allen asked for on the shelves, such as a loaf of bread. As they were leaving, Allen realised he needed money from the cash machine outside. With sunlight shining on the glass screen making it difficult for Allen to see, and with the money and receipt slot set far up the back of the machine, Allen was struggling. Suddenly without being asked, Endal jumped up to retrieve the card and money when Allen had made his transaction.

Newspaper photographers asked him to do it again and again, so they could get their pictures. This was the photograph that was used when Endal was voted 'Dog of the Millennium' in the *Dogs Today* competition. The result was that Endal was splashed over nearly every front page. The press went wild and reporters from around the world wanted to know

Top: Well, that's one way of chopping tomatoes!

Bottom: Endal getting some cash

Opposite: Crufts, and Endal shows off his PDSA Gold Medal

about this extraordinary dog. He was filmed by crews almost daily. People started to recognise the yellow Labrador as 'Endal, the Cashpoint Dog'.

Meanwhile, miraculously, Allen's speech was improving dramatically and his twitching had almost stopped. Indeed, to hear him now, it's hard to believe that once it was almost incomprehensible, despite 5 years of speech therapy. Neither Allen nor Sandra is certain how Endal achieved this, although Allen thinks it was because he desperately wanted to talk back to a dog who obviously loved him so much. Even more touching, Endal talks too. 'He has twenty different voice patterns,' Allen tells us. 'The tone can mean all kinds of things, ranging from "I love you" to "Can't we switch television channels?"' (His favourite programmes involve anything with animals!)

Allen lifts Endal onto his knee to tickle his huge tummy and demonstrate how he 'talks'. Endal looks up at his master adoringly and howls with pleasure. The noise is so loud that one half expects someone to knock on Allen's front door to see what's going on. In actual fact the neighbours are used to it. Allen and his dog are well known in Clanfield. Because of his poor memory, which means Allen can usually only remember things for 48 hours, he also forgets people's names and faces. Before Endal came into his life, Allen was too embarrassed to go out much or talk to friends who could remember him, since often he had no idea who they were. 'Now, they come up to talk about Endal and, even if I don't know who they are, Endal provides a talking point. They stroke and chat, which helps me to socialise again.'

Endal has also helped Allen's marriage and the relationship with his children, Liam, now 16, and Zoe, 15. 'They all love him (even though Endal very obviously prefers me!). He sleeps on my side of the bed, touching my wheelchair with his paw and when Sandra and I sit on the sofa, watching television, he jumps up between us.'

Sandra, an amazing woman who has put up with more than most wives could cope with, accepts this. 'Life will never be the same again but thanks to Endal, Allen has a second chance – and so do we. Out of 80 seriously injured married men in the Gulf War, only eight marriages survived. Ours is one of them. The children lost their old dad, but now Endal has given them a new one.' As Allen's confidence grew, his ability to speak began to re-emerge. Encouraged into trying words with Endal, it was as though the links to his dormant speech memory were awakened by his desire to communicate again. Today, Allen's main problem, in contrast to his previous inability to speak, is letting people get a word in edgeways!

However the most moving example of Endal's initiative happened in May 2001, when the pair were invited to attend Crufts. After checking into

the hotel the night before, Allen took Endal outside for a run across a green on the other side of the hotel car park. As usual his lead was clipped to the chair. Suddenly a vehicle reversed towards them. Endal was between Allen and the car so, instinctively, Allen pushed the dog out of the way. Seconds later, the car knocked the chair over and Allen blacked out. When he came round, he found Endal pulling his body over, using his teeth on his jacket. The dog then ran back for his mobile phone, which he got out of the bag and thrust against his face. Endal began barking for help.

The story hit the national headlines. Endal, it appeared, was the first dog ever to put a human into the equivalent of the recovery position, without being taught. Once again he was a familiar face on the television and in the news. Everyone wanted footage of this remarkable dog.

Endal's resolve and quiet control, following Allen's second shunt with a vehicle, made headline news and won him that most prestigious of animal awards – the PDSA Gold Medal – the animal equivalent of the George Cross, for his astonishing response. The citation reads: "For Devotion to Duty and Animal Bravery". In 2002, HRH Princess Alexandra presented Endal with his Medal, awarded to animals that have shown outstanding devotion to their duties in time of peace, and he became one of the first three dogs, at the time, ever to receive the Medal. (It is perhaps worth noting here, that the Charity Canine Partners is the *only* UK dog organisation to have two such Gold Medals awarded to its dogs.)

Endal has also been awarded a Gold *Blue Peter* Badge (the second dog ever to receive this award).

And what of Allen – a serviceman whose only wish was proudly to serve Queen and country? Having recently had the honour of meeting HM The Queen at Windsor Castle, Allen Parton confessed whilst there that he still has a feeling of guilt about coming home injured. Indeed it was his belief that he had let his Queen, his family and his country down. He was told in no uncertain terms that it was foolish for him to feel this way, but it is possible the burden of guilt will never leave this very proud man.

Right: Endal - the old sea-dog

Below: Allen & Endal visit M&S

Opposite: Allen & Endal have a quick cuddle

Endal's achievements to date

2005	Runner hope *Hero Dog of the Year* (Crufts 2005)
2004	*Lifetime Achievement Award* (Wag and Bone Show)
2002	PDSA *Gold Medal* – equivalent of The George Cross awarded to animals that have shown outstanding devotion to their duties in peace time.
2002	Endal became the first Assistance dog to be awarded the Kennel Club's *Gold Good Citizen* award, presented to him at Crufts 2002
2002	Presented with the first ever 'Lifetime Achievement' Award at the *Golden Bone Awards*
2001/2	*Assistance Dog of the Year* Award
2001	*Local Hero* Award
2000	*Dog of the Millennium* (named by *Dogs Today*)
2000	Prodog '*Dog of the Year*' Award

In 2004, Allen and Endal where both awarded a Life-time Achievement Award at the annual Wag and Bone Show.

Endal himself hates to be parted from Allen. When Sandra and Allen took a skiing holiday recently, Endal had to go to kennels. As Allen picked him up, he gave him a muted lick, but as soon as they got home and closed the front door, he leaped up at him with slobbery kisses. 'Men like us dislike public shows of affection!' jokes Allen.

Endal is also a well-seasoned traveller and a regular on British Rail, when travelling with Allen to charity events or TV studios. BR always reserves 2 seats for him and once, when delayed at Waterloo, he put on an impromptu show of fetching and carrying for commuters, who as a result were reluctant to go, even when their train arrived.

And so.....

Sandra and Allen have since been re-married. Allen says: 'At long last I feel the final bit of the puzzle is now in place. I now feel married to this very special lady whom I have fallen in love with again. Endal was my best man.' For the record, Endal appeared in a matching gold waistcoat to the one worn by Allen!

'When Mum and Dad got remarried, it was such a fantastic day as we finally became a real family again and Liam and I finally got our Dad back,' confirms now 19-year-old daughter Zoe. 'Before Endal arrived, Dad never wanted to go out and could hardly talk. He was like a stranger to us and now that has all changed.'

So what then?

A lifetime lost? Not at all! Apart from encouraging Allen to learn to talk again, Endal has helped Allen rebuild his life and that of his family. There is also the 'fame' issue, which prevents any possibility of Allen backsliding into feeling sorry for himself. A dog as talented as Endal is a difficult secret to keep. Reporters and film crews from around the world have queued up to watch and marvel as Endal, wallet in mouth, picks up Allen's prescription at the chemist's, or operates the electronic doors on a train. Amazingly, the total number of film-crews from all around the world that have filmed Endal now numbers over 300!

Allen is also confident that Endal's cute face, as well as his life-transforming qualities, have already helped to bring many disability issues to light, including improvements in public transport, wheelchair access, grants to help people care for their assistance dogs and the importance of being seen as a 'person' rather than just 'a person in a wheelchair'.

'My hope is that more injured service personnel hear about the benefits of assistance dogs,' he adds. 'The majority of partnerships have stemmed from word of mouth and personal recommendation and for those that are suffering alone, I want them to know that these dogs can make the difference between merely existing and living a real life.' *(Of course, this holds good for people in all walks of life.)*

'People with disabilities often think they are either too well, or too ill, to have an assistance dog and I just say 'go for it'. The physiological benefits of having a dog, or indeed any animal, are only starting to be understood and I think I am testament to how powerful the effect can be.'

At last year's *Crufts*, where the pair came runners-up in the Kennel Club's *Hero Dog Award* in front of an audience of 17 million, Allen says he felt prouder of Endal than ever before. 'We were both there under that spotlight against all odds and I felt tears welling that this could be our last *Crufts* together, as a working team. There may come a time when Endal himself decides to hang up his working jacket, but that does not stop his enabling me from the moment I wake, until my head hits the pillow at night.'

The future

Endal is now 9 years old. There will come a time when he will be too old to carry out his duties, however strong and faithful the urge to do so. When that happens, Allen will be there to look after him, repaying what he acknowledges to be a debt that can never be repaid. 'I am going to look after him,' says Allen. 'When he retires, I shall ask to keep him and we shall grow old, disgracefully, together!'

'Of course the day will come when I lower my hand down by my side and Endal won't be there physically,' say Allen, 'but in spirit he will always be beside me and his legacy will outlive all of us. When I finally arrive at the pearly gates myself, I know in my heart of hearts that Endal will be there waiting faithfully for me with his otter-like tail in full swing.'

Right: Endal – hero dog, Crufts 2004

When looking at what Endal has achieved for Allen Parton, we are probably filled with wonder that a 'simple dog' can transform someone's life in this way. How is it possible for a dog not only to learn such things, but also continue to develop, in a similar way to that expected of children? There follows a short story, as true as it is astounding, about another young dog, who saved his human partner's life.

In order for dogs to work with people with limited movement or mobility, they need to be highly motivated. They need to enjoy the work and the work needs to be rewarding, because they cannot be coerced into doing anything. They will work off lead inside the house and may even need to put on their own lead and collar. They also may need to take off their own lead for free exercise in the park, or to call the lift in a shopping centre or hospital. By introducing 'errorless learning' and problem solving to puppies in weekly training classes, they develop a positive attitude to any form of learning. The pay-off for the human handler is that the dog associates learning as an activity with a powerful sense of achievement and excitement, so they are highly motivated to work out ways to help humans in daily life activities.

ORCA'S STORY – 'GET HELP'

> *'Nothing much comes between Orca and food … except me.'* (Cheryl Smith)

Cheryl Smith graduated with Canine Partner Orca, following a two-week residential training course, at the end of March 2003. Once she and Orca successfully completed all the training, testing and assessment, they went home and began to work together as a partnership. Orca, by working so readily for Cheryl, showed that he had 'chosen' her as someone he preferred to be with. This rapport was strengthened during the difficult and challenging training course and further developed once they began encountering real-life situations.

Anybody who doesn't know what soap tastes like, never washed a dog.
—Franklin P. Jones

Cheryl & Orca Graduation

Cheryl & Orca enjoying spring time

Among the tasks taught to Orca at the Canine Partners training centre in Midhurst, West Sussex, was to notice if one of the trainers had fallen from the wheelchair, and then to get the phone and to lie beside the trainer until he/she moved or help arrived. This is significant when we learn what unfolded that rainy, wintry day in York, only eight weeks later. One other test we will train our puppies for is to allow themselves to be taken by the collar by a stranger, so that in a hospital or a medical emergency the dog can be held whilst people are dealing with the Partner's crisis.

However this was the last thing on Cheryl's mind as she set out in the wind and rain to exercise Orca in the deserted playing fields near the University – and then disaster struck. Her wheelchair hit a rock in the mud, slipped sideways and then careered down to the bottom of a running creek, trapping Cheryl underneath 300lbs of powered wheelchair, her head barely above water. Now this is already a dangerous situation for anybody, but for Cheryl it was doubly critical, because her medical condition meant that she not only couldn't move at all to get the wheelchair off her, or crawl out from under it, but also she suffers from poor circulation. This dramatically increased the risk of her going into hypothermia and suffering a medical crisis. If help didn't arrive soon, Cheryl's life was at stake.

Orca immediately tried to respond as taught, and tried to climb down the bank towards her. Cheryl knew that, comforting though this would be, it wouldn't help her, so she had to try to send him away from her, even though she was clearly in distress and helpless. Using the verbal signals taught to her on her CP training course, Cheryl directed him with her voice to move away up the bank and keep going. Whispering to him: 'Get help' and then using voice commands to reinforce any movements he made away rather than towards her, she desperately tried to make him understand that he needed to go somewhere and do something, rather than stay with her.

Suddenly he seemed to get the idea and darted off into the rain. As she lay there in the water, freezing cold, shivering and helpless, she wondered if the dog was doing anything more than just playing in the park, or worse, just wandering off into the streets of York.

Orca in a paddling pool

He had only ever encountered this situation, in training, so she had no idea what he would understand or do. She and Orca had only been together for two months, so she wasn't really sure whether there was enough of a bond for the dog to try to help her. After what seemed ages, he suddenly arrived back at her side, muddy and without his collar.

'Oh no, he's just been playing,' she groaned, and feebly directed him to get help. Again he tried to get to her, but then suddenly seemed to understand and sprang back up the bank and off into the distance. Meanwhile Cheryl was drifting in and out of consciousness and any hope of being found in the rain, the wind and the dark empty playing fields was rapidly fading. And the water was rising.

'Are you alright?' A man's voice startled her back to her senses and she weakly called out 'Help me.' Being unable to shift the chair, her unknown rescuer rushed off again to summon the Fire Brigade, which arrived promptly with a crane to lift the wheelchair off Cheryl and retrieve her from her freezing bath in the creek. Cheryl was rushed to hospital, with advanced hypothermia, all the time asking where Orca was.

It subsequently turned out that the man who found her was a jogger, who didn't particularly like dogs! However he said that this Golden Retriever, muddy and collarless, rushed up to him and jumped up and down in front of him and then ran back, towards Cheryl. The dog repeated this action until finally the jogger felt that he should follow the dog and see what was up. Only when he peered down into the murky storm drain, did he realise that someone was down there, trapped under a wheelchair in the water and – being unable to shift the heavy chair himself – he rushed to call the Fire Brigade and Ambulance.

When she was released from hospital, Cheryl was reunited with Orca and went home to recover. It was when she was checking her phone messages that the whole extraordinary picture of what Orca had been up to finally became clear. The message said, 'Hi. I found your dog wandering loose in the park, got your number from his collar and tried to put him in the car to bring him back to you. I am sorry, but he struggled

Above left: Mud, glorious mud!

Above right: Orca relaxing: every now and again you have to stop and smell the flowers!

and resisted me, and then slipped the collar and ran off, so I have no idea where he is now. I have your dog's collar if you want to collect it.' She later met the man and got the full story from him.

Orca hadn't just been off having a wonderful time playing in the mud. He had been running for miles, looking for someone. When he met this man exercising his dog in the playing fields, he ran up to him eagerly. But when the man took hold of his collar and tried to lead him into the car (remember we had trained him to do this in an emergency), he struggled wildly and broke free of the man. Going against his training, he ran off again and back to Cheryl. The second time he finally found someone, he did his best to indicate to the jogger to follow him, to go where the dog was 'pointing'. He did this well enough that the man, who did not know anything about dogs or dog behaviour, recognised that the dog was clearly trying to tell him something.

On so many levels this was an extraordinary achievement for Orca. For him to go against his training and actually leave the side of the person he was supposed to stay with and to assist, was a major conflict for a sensitive and obedient Golden Retriever. Then to refuse to allow himself to be taken by a stranger, but later to allow himself to be taken quietly to the Police station by one of the attending officers, showed that he was able to discriminate between allowing this action, when it was appropriate and resisting when it was not appropriate. The action of getting the attention of the jogger was one he initiated himself. It was not based upon any previous training and is not a behaviour that frequently occurs between dogs and people, although it may occur between some dogs, or within some breeds.

Finally, on the most fundamental level, the dog acted to save a person whom he had known for only eight weeks. For most of us this is such a crucial point – what motivates a dog to do this, rather than just to go off and play in the park? Dog clubs and training classes are full of dogs that run off and don't come back when they are called. There are so many distractions and interesting smells to investigate and most dogs do not get enough opportunities to just run and run and sniff and play. So whenever they get a chance, they take off and the owner may not see them for hours. Anytime one of our Canine Partners is in a crisis, where the owner has fallen, is unconscious, or helpless, the dog is free.

There is absolutely nothing to prevent the dog from just taking off down the street to raid garbage bins, or into the park or the woods or the forest to roll in fox pooh, chase rabbits, or just splash about in puddles. So why does the dog choose to try to help?

There is no 'survival value', as the scientists like to say, from a dog's point of view, which would prompt it to go and get help for a weak or injured partner. Dogs are scavengers by nature and development, so they are cooperative but also competitive. Our Canine Partners dogs have always been fed regularly, have always been praised, rewarded, played with and taken

ORCA receives his PDSA Gold Medal for devotion to duty, with proud Partner Cheryl Smith; behind (L-R): AP Alexander, Marilyn Rydstrom CEO PDSA, Nicky Pendleton SROT – a Founder and Vice Chairman of Canine Partners, Freddie Bircher – Chairman PDSA and Terry Knott, CEO of Canine Partners

care of. They are assured of love and care regardless of what they do, so the act of going against training to actively assist someone is a choice.

Orca was awarded the PDSA Gold Medal (often referred to as the canine George Cross), to recognise and acknowledge the efforts he made to keep his new human partner safe.

We may never know why a dog goes to such lengths, but this is one aspect of the human–animal bond that speaks to us all and resonates for us. He is, at the end of the day, just a sweet dog, who has been trained to work proactively with humans and solve problems. The unconditional support and love, reflected in his actions, reassures us that respect and kindness are essential in the way we should behave towards all animals, because they are capable of giving back so much more, if given half a chance.

Today Cheryl has successfully passed her Masters degree at University, and she and Orca are a real team. It could have been so different, were it not for this extraordinary dog and his devotion to duty.

Cheryl & Orca: Wag & Bone Award

2005

Chapter THREE

A Tale of Two Dogs – Whose Career Paths Changed Dramatically

'A dog is the only thing on earth that loves you more than he loves himself.'
—Josh Billings

Part 1

JERRY LEE – Police Dog

As I crouched on top of the workbench, keeping as still as possible, I tried to carefully angle my head to see what the Police Officer was doing. He was intently tapping in notes on a hand-held computer, absorbed in his task. Then, with exaggerated slowness and stealth, the officer turned to look back into the room. He too, was seated on top of a workbench, and he too was trying to keep as still as possible so that he didn't draw attention to himself.

What was prowling around the room below us, keeping us trapped up there? The creature was wolf-grey, with a pitch black face, and huge paws, sniffing and checking out every corner of the area. Part of the tail had a ring of hair missing. We exchanged glances – and gave each other the thumbs up sign. Then the Police Officer, Steve Dean, quietly slipped down onto the floor and crouched – ready for the moment when the animal turned and noticed him. At that instant, Steve clapped his hands. The creature stopped, stared at him, and then ran forward, leaping on him and trying to wrestle him to the ground.

This is not a scene from a horror movie, but Test Number 2 for any German Shepherd puppy hoping to become a Police dog, for the Metropolitan Police Dog section. These puppies are seven weeks of age, and Steve is running a routine assessment procedure of each one, to determine whether they will be placed with a Police dog handler, or trained for explosives detection, or re-homed with one of the families on the waiting list for a rejected puppy. Our puppy showed the attitude and athleticism to be an excellent Police dog and was passed as suitable.

By hiding from the puppy, when it is first brought into an unfamiliar area, we can see how confidently the puppy will deal with this potentially stressful or frightening event. When the Tester appears, we can see how readily the puppy will approach a stranger and be prepared to make contact and interact. By observing these and many other responses to the various tests that Dean uses, he can select puppies with potential for a working life and place them with an appropriate handler. Puppies that are too appeasing, or quiet, or unsure of themselves, will be more likely to be placed with families. Steve has invited me to watch how he assesses puppies and then he will later watch whilst I assess some Golden Retriever puppies on their aptitude for assistance dog work.

He invites me to assess a few of his German Shepherd puppies. Then a small, dark puppy enters the room. He peers around, sits and gazes for a minute, then very carefully checks the immediate vicinity before sitting down again. He stays calm and quiet and listens to the noises in the background. When I hop down off the work bench and clap hands, the puppy is hesitant to approach, then creeps forward, wagging his tail appeasingly, and he licks my hands. The puppy responds in the same way to all the tests – gentle, interested, appeasing, wanting to stay with me, happy to retrieve the teaspoon, not willing to tug too hard on the toy, and generally showing an agreeable, sweet nature.

Steve shrugs, shakes his head and puts him on the list of reject puppies for waiting families, but I am still playing with this dear little puppy. 'Steve – this little chap would make an ideal assistance dog. He is perfect. These are the sort of responses we really look for.' But Steve explains that there is a long list of people; some have been waiting for a couple of years. I am disappointed but I have to accept the situation. After the testing is completed and we are walking back to the office, Steve turns to me and says: 'Oh all right – take him. Try him out as a Canine Partner.'

And that was the way that Jerry Lee entered our training programme. Our first German Shepherd Dog, he grew from being a funny, dark, weedy-looking puppy into one of the most handsome of dogs. The rich gold markings, coupled with the slightly long, dense black coat and his gorgeous face and expression made him a real pin-up boy with the puppy parents and members of the public. His puppy parent, Judith, dressed him up as Red Riding Hood for the end-of-year Puppy Party at Canine Partners and he won a prize.

The training went well for him – he enjoyed learning and was easily able to do the various aspects of assistance dog work – from tugging doors open, to pressing switches, and paying at the check-out. A typical Shepherd, he adored his puppy parent, and would do anything for her. The downside of this is that he found it difficult to be parted from her, and struggled with the initial stages of advanced training, when he had to come into the Training Centre each day and work with the trainers. He would constantly watch out for Judith and if she came into the centre, he would scream if he heard her voice. This made life difficult for the trainers (none of us likes being rejected!) but it meant that he would bond wonderfully with the potential disabled person.

He was also a puppy with a delicate system – often unwell, we had to be very careful about the food and the type of treats that he received and there were many times when we wondered if he would be stable enough to be placed as an assistance dog. But he was an entertaining dog and we could make jokes during demonstrations because he made such a noise when he was enthusiastically opening the washing machine – whining, and yipping. We said that he was a typical male and hated doing the washing!

Finally, he was ready to be partnered with someone. Ann arrived at the training centre, having applied for an assistance dog. Knowing nothing about dogs, she was expecting to try out with some gentle little Golden Retrievers. So she was suitably appalled when confronted with this glamorous beast! I forgot to mention that he was not only good looking – he also grew very large.

His coat was dense and long, and his feet and legs were thick and powerful, so that his appearance was actually rather intimidating to someone seated down low in a manual wheelchair.

Ann was very dubious about the prospect of working with Jerry Lee, but he almost immediately decided that she was the person he had been waiting for. He was like butter in her hands and she had just the right combination of authority and humour to bring out the best in him.

Gradually over the ensuing assessment days, Ann and Jerry became 'an item' and were invited to attend

Jerry Lee

Going to Garden Party at Buckingham Palace

The big bad wolf (alias Jerry Lee) with puppy parent Judith Warner

Left: Jerry Lee grew very large!

Opposite page: Jerry Lee as a puppy

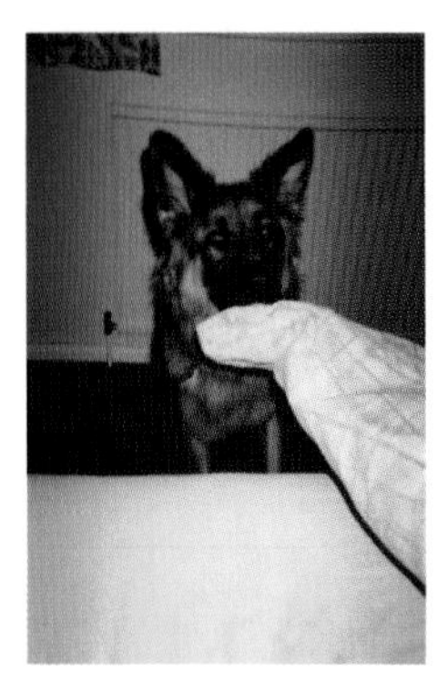
Jerry Lee makes the bed

the Canine Partners residential training course. This entails two weeks in the Holton Lee respite centre based in Poole, Dorset, learning how to live and work together, how to communicate with each other and for Ann, most importantly, how to manoeuvre around the constant cluster of admirers, desperate to touch and stroke the handsome beast trotting so attentively beside her.

Of course they graduated effortlessly, but the transition to home and work was not without hiccups. Ann had to deal with the fact that Jerry Lee, like so many Shepherds, tended to bark if he was uncertain about a situation or a person. This had a terrifying effect on bystanders and Ann needed to work really hard to find ways to reassure people that Jerry was a '*cuddlepot*' and not a killer!

Her learning curve was immense. Not only did she have to learn about dog behaviour, training, management, care, and control, but she also had to learn about dealing with members of the public who either wanted to hug and kiss Jerry Lee, or scream and run from him.

They developed into a seamless partnership. Jerry Lee accompanied her to work and helped her throughout the day, opening heavy doors, getting things for her, taking things to other people, and sharing the extremes of British weather! They went on outings, trips and long country walks, and this 'failed' Police dog was able to show people the caring side of the German Shepherd. It is extraordinary how well a dog may adapt so closely to one particular human being, so that he becomes virtually a part of that person. The two were inseparable, and they brought out the best in each other. Both Ann and Canine Partners will always be grateful for Steve Dean and the Metropolitan Police dog breeding programme, for making it possible for Jerry Lee to join the ranks of assistance dogs, yet again changing the way we think about the human–dog relationship.

Part 2

YUKON – Canine Partner to 'Rover Response Dog' – or Super-Sense Me!

When detecting drugs, explosives, human remains and DVDs, the dog has something very physical to search for. Human trainers train the dogs by placing the substance in various locations and rewarding the dog for finding the substance and indicating the location to the trainer.

But how do you train a dog to detect something that a human cannot see, hear, smell or detect even with any sort of human equipment?

Although researchers now agree that dogs may occasionally be able to alert to the fact that a person is about to experience an epileptic fit, they have no way of verifying what the dog is alerting to, or how the dog knew that this event was about to happen. Since Seizure Alert dogs (and cats) seem to be able to detect seizures up to an hour before they happen, the researchers are now trying to establish just exactly what is being sensed; and how.

There have been various research projects based upon the premise that the dog is alerting to a smell, but as yet, nothing has been proved. In the meantime, organisations such as Canine Partners, and Paws with a Cause in the USA, have side-stepped the issue, by teaching the dogs to respond appropriately and helpfully when a person experiences a fit or seizure. By teaching the dogs what to do and how to do it reliably for rewards, the trainers can place Seizure Response or Emergency Response dogs with people who fit a defined profile of seizure activity.

Mysteriously, in practice, many dogs begin to alert before the person actually experiences the seizure.

Left: Yukon (centre) and friends

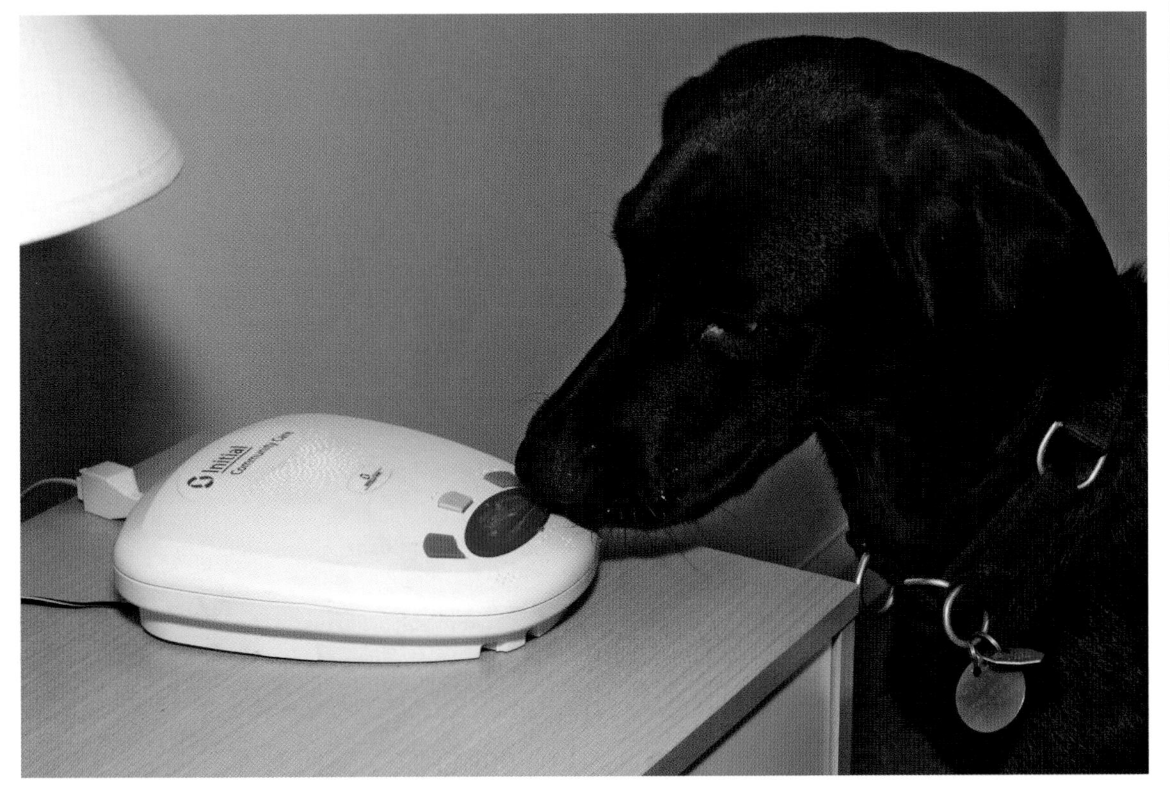

Left: Yukon pressing the emergency button in the home

As the dog already knows what to do and is safely trained in response procedure, the dog is not as stressed by an epileptic fit, as an untrained dog would be. Therefore the dog is able to utilise the extraordinary canine capacity for observation, memory and association, and to notice the subtle changes that begin to occur long before the physical symptoms impact on the person.

Seizure Response dogs can gradually change, to become Seizure Alert dogs, through their own volition and inclination. It would be impossible to teach dogs to alert to something that the trainer does not know will happen. Yet by training the dogs in how they can help a person in that situation, it appears the dogs are able to teach themselves what to look for and then take preventative steps to assist the person to find a safe place and get assistance if needed.

When Yukon arrived at Canine Partners, he was very gentle, sensitive and sweet. Completely the opposite of the sibling trainees – wild boys Wizard and Wombat, or the 'tomboy' Izzie – he was more of a poet than a soldier. This is the sort of temperament that usually makes an excellent assistance dog, so he started his puppy classes with great promise.

As a young Black Labrador Retriever, he was expected to go through a 'delinquent' stage as he matured, but instead, he seemed to become even more sensitive and reactive. This characteristic could have been a liability if he had been placed as a Canine Partner, required to go into busy, noisy shopping centres, cope with crowded lifts and bustling shoppers, because such a life would possibly be stressful for him.

However such a temperament and personality can actually be ideal for a very different sort of placement, so the trainers at Canine Partners began to investigate whether he could be trained as an emergency response dog. Although all Canine Partners dogs are trained in a basic emergency response, some dogs are required to carry out this function on a regular basis. If a person's condition causes dizzy spells, collapses, blackouts, or seizures, the dog needs to be more specifically trained how to cope and what to do to help.

A couple had applied to become Puppy Parents, but the man had suffered a brain haemorrhage and as a result, had impaired movement and speech and experienced frequent epileptic seizures. Previously he had been a successful professional – a vet with a busy practice, but his condition had now deteriorated and he struggled to cope with life outside the home. His wife was strongly supportive, but the situation required her to be attentive to her husband all the time. Effectively, she had to give up her independent life to be a personal assistant to him, whilst taking over the running and management of their lives. Such a situation is always exhausting and stressful.

The trainers then set up an assessment of Yukon for his possible reactions to the sights and sounds of someone having an epileptic seizure, by mimicking the pattern of the fit. Such an approach had been pioneered by Paws with a Cause in the USA and it is an essential step, if a dog is being considered for placement with anyone who suffers seizures.

The behaviour change in a person undergoing a seizure can be dramatic and unnerving to a dog and many dogs are indeed terrified. Whilst most dogs will try to get away, some may actually bite the person, or become terribly stressed and try to avoid the person as much as possible. Others can completely misread the situation, deciding that the person wants to play a game of rough and tumble – the dog may pounce on the person, grab and tear at their body or clothes, or leap around them, barking furiously. Others just try to pretend that the person doesn't exist and will wander around the room, studiously avoiding any glances at the person.

Yukon is a sensitive and reactive fellow, easily spooked by noises or unfamiliar situations, and yet he immediately went to the trainer circled around him sniffing and licking him, and then went and got a toy and stood near him – gazing at him. Then he lay down at the trainer's head and licked his face. All of these responses indicated that Yukon would try to nurture the person rather than hurt him, so this gave the trainers a green light to go ahead with the training.

He had to learn the first signs of an impending seizure and those signs would become his cue to press the emergency alarm phone. He had to also learn to get help from the man's wife, by finding her and indicating in a particular way that she had been taught, to recognise as a sign that her own intervention was

needed. Yukon had already learned some standard emergency responses, such as bringing a blanket and a mobile phone, but he had to learn the specifics of this situation and his new home.

Dogs are wonderful observers of each other and of people – it is of course a survival mechanism in the wild. They can quickly learn to 'back-chain events' – in other words, they can learn that the sound of a particular TV soap's theme tune will trigger various people to rush to the kitchen, pour a cup of tea and then hurry back to settle down on the settee for half an hour. Or they can learn the dreaded words: 'He needs a bath!', and go and hide in the garden. Or more simply, they can learn that the rattle of the car keys at a certain time of day means: 'We are going to the park!'

Yukon soon learned to notice the tiniest changes in his new owner's face, body, movements and emotions and is now able to pinpoint with great accuracy when a seizure is likely to occur. This is reassuring for the husband, but it is also incredibly liberating for the wife, because she can relax, leave the house for short periods of time and get back some of her life. The fact that her husband is safe, has an attentive and responsible companion and that she can be alerted if she is needed, gives her extraordinary peace of mind.

The interesting aspect to this story is that what could have been a liability (Yukon's sensitivity, his tendency to react with anxiety to unfamiliar events, and his need to be with people) has turned into the greatest gift he could give to a human being. What prevented him from being a busy, active Canine Partner, has enabled him to utilise those qualities in a very specific way and assist his new partner to achieve a more positive and proactive life.

Because he knows exactly what to do and he feels safe and loved in this situation, Yukon's self-confidence has blossomed. His job includes all the retrieving and assistance dog tasks of any Canine Partner, along with his special task of Seizure Response. Both he and his owner are now able to visit confidently and be out in public and so get on with their lives. This is a mutually beneficial placement (as indeed are all the Canine Partners teams). The dog feels safe and secure in the knowledge that he knows how to help and cope with his owner's condition; and his owner knows he can cope with more of life, because his constant and vigilant companion will be waiting to assist if necessary.

The use of dogs to alert for seizures has captured the imagination of the press and the public, but it is important to recognise how stressful such a job can be for any dog. It is essential to find the right dog for the job, because it can so easily go dangerously wrong. Finally many people who have seizures do not have the type or frequency that can be effectively helped by a dog, but when assessed and chosen with care, a kind, and gentle dog like Yukon may be able to help.

Left: Yukon assessed for reaction to fake seizure

Chapter FOUR

Nose Jobs – Izzie, Wombat and Wizard – 'The Nose Knows'

Dogs are assisting humans in many new ways that rely upon the dog's almost unimaginable capacity to detect minute differences in the molecules that make up scent patterns.

'There is no psychiatrist in the world like a puppy licking your face.'
—Ben Williams

The airport security queues are long; people are crowded together and tense. As they wait impatiently, a dog with a uniformed handler seems to wander casually along the lines of people. Then a different type of dog appears, actively bustling in and out of the people. Around the back in Baggage Handling, several different dogs are at work, checking all the luggage and items. Meanwhile, outside the airport in the car park, police and Forensic Investigators are working in cooperation with yet another type of dog, which is intently examining, inch by inch, a cordoned off area that is a possible crime scene.

International travellers are now familiar with the sight of Beagles checking their luggage for illegal foodstuffs. Many are also aware that 'Drugs Dogs' check their baggage in the airport. What they may not realise is that other dogs, trained to detect a range of other substances, are now operational in many countries.

Because the canine brain has a large proportion dedicated to analysing and remembering the components of scents, dogs are able to detect minute similarities and differences in substances. The trick is to teach them what we want them to detect, and then train them to do so willingly, eagerly and very reliably.

Dogs are great at 'Match to Sample'. They can sniff a hair follicle that has been stored in formaldehyde for three years, and match it to the right person in a line-up of people. Canine Hard-nosed Evidence is being used in courts of law in Europe; extensive testing and evaluation for reliability has been done on how dogs recognise the differences that the human handler cannot detect. Dogs are being deployed in many ways due to this capacity and also to the new methods of training that allow handlers to tell the dog what to search for. Examples are:

- Termite, fungus, mould detection (insurance work)
- Fire accelerant detection (Fire Brigade and services) (see ex-Canine Partner Izzie below)
- Drugs (Police)
- Explosives and firearms (British Transport, anti-terrorism) (see ex-Canine Partner Wombat below)
- Money, DVDs, illegal foodstuffs (Customs)
- Illegal animal and agricultural imports (customs)
- Low blood sugar alert (medical emergency)
- Seizure alert and response (medical emergency) (see Chapter 3)

Crime Scene Investigation dog

- Crime Scene Investigation – blood detection, human remains (Forensic Science) *(see also Chapter 5)*

In this chapter we will showcase several different types of dogs that are now being used by law enforcement agencies. The first dogs started life hoping to grow up to be a Canine Partners assistance dog, but their special talents and skills were recognised and they were streamed into completely different careers.

Izzie – The 'New Age' Fire Dog

Headlines: 'Fire Investigation Dog aids Investigators'

The use of dogs for the purposes of Fire Investigation (FI) was first established in the USA in 1987. Responding to an upsurge in the annual number of arson cases reported nationally, the Federal Department of Alcohol Tobacco and Firearms (ATF), whose responsibility it is in the USA to combat these national trends, undertook feasibility trials in partnership with the Connecticut State Fire Marshal's Office. So successful were these early trials that an expanded training and development programme was established, resulting in the first trained and certified dogs being deployed operationally during 1989.

The use of FI dogs is now widely accepted as a major benefit to the Fire Investigator in locating traces of ignitable liquids remaining at any fire scene under investigation. There are now many hundreds of FI Dogs in regular use in both the USA and Canada, whilst other dogs are currently being utilised in both Australia and South Africa with equal success. Even though it seems unbelievable when you see a pet dog pottering about in the garden, these dogs are able to work in extremes of heat, dirt, chemicals, pools of water and building debris.

However, the use of FI Dogs in the UK is a relatively new development. Investigation and research into the subject was carried out by (then) Sub-Officer Peplow of Lancashire Fire and Rescue Service during 1993–1996 based largely on the work already undertaken in the USA and Australia. Dave Peplow developed the Lancashire FI dog facility in close co-operation with Lancashire Fire and Rescue Service. As he says, 'I am extremely proud of the fact that I have been privileged to train both dogs and handlers for many of the Fire Services, as well as delivering continuation training for other dogs.'

Meanwhile back at Canine Partners, a lively, intense black Labrador named Xie (pronounced 'Ixy') was being assessed for her potential as a future assistance dog. Both clever and eager, she was a delight to train, but other less inviting aspects of her character made us think seriously about whether life as a Canine Partner would be best for her. She loved to chase balls and would hunt them down long after the game was finished. This obsessive desire to play and chase is undesirable for a dog which must stay calm and attentive at all times to their owner.

Not only that, Xie thought she was the toughest kid on the block, and spent a lot of her time trying to

Izzie

prove this to other dogs. Chasing them, pinning them down, arguing about who owns the ball and throwing her weight around, Xie just wasn't the most fun to be around other dogs. As a Canine Partner, she would need to be extra tolerant of other dogs in public, so we eventually realised that this was her nature and that as such, she really wasn't suited to the job of assistance dog.

So we contacted Dave Peplow and asked him to assess her for the job of hunting down something a little different – the accelerants that have been used to start fires. During the assessment, she was a little star, flying around the place and thrilled to be allowed to just sniff and run as much as she wanted.

However, her strong character began to surface during training. As Dave says: 'A number of problems developed during training – firstly she would not/could not indicate in the way I wanted.' Ideally the dog should freeze and stay very still to pinpoint the location of the substance, but she was so quick to learn and do, that she learned the wrong thing and they struggled to change it back. However, she eventually

Izzie does the biz!

learned that lying down with her nose right on top of the scent source was the only way she could earn her reward. Now she does this so well that on one of her first operational searches involving a double murder/ arson, she was first required to search a suspect couple's house, then do an area clearance in the streets around the fire scene following which, whilst finally searching the murder/fire scene, she located what later proved to be petrol behind the front door of the property.

Also despite her lack of concentration during training (she would make a couple of finds, and then 'switch off'), once she actually became operational and starting searching real fire scenes, she began to show what she was capable of. Now that she has worked a number of 'live' fire scenes, she switches on at the first scent of fire damage and will quite literally drag the handler down the street to reach the fire scene. This reveals how much she is tuning in with the handler – she notices how differently he reacts when things are 'for real', so she changes to her intense and focussed 'mind on the job' attitude.

She is now called Izzie (apparently it is easier to say!) and is generally a lovely little dog. However her little character quirks still show up when she interacts with other dogs. Off lead, she will run over and greet other dogs, but returns instantly when whistled. On lead, if she meets a strange dog, her whole attitude changes, and she will reveal that less attractive side where she feels obliged to threaten and growl to keep them away from her. Fortunately she is excellent around sheep, mainly because she is frightened of them! At home in the kennels she plays very hard and is quite rough with the other dogs, trying to make up for her rather petite size.

Fortunately, being charming to other dogs is not part of the remit for a FI dog! So, this little street-wise kid has come a long way from being rejected as a Canine Partner. Now fulfilling a demanding and incredibly useful job for humans, she is able to be herself, play hard and work hard and live her life to the full. As Dave says: 'She ranks as one of the most "characterful" dogs that we have ever had the pleasure to work with over the years!'

WOMBAT and WIZARD – Canine Crime-Fighting Duo

Even though the yellow Labrador-Golden Retriever cross dog Wombat doesn't realise that 2006 was the Chinese Year of the Dog, he has abilities that are incredibly valuable in any year. Wombat was chosen to be 'the Face of British Transport Police' for their Year of the Dog recruitment posters. Admittedly he is a cute dog, and very photogenic, but his work is usually down away from the bright lights and cameras.

Wombat and his handler, Sgt Peter Wanless, are employed by the British Transport Police (BTP) Explosive Search Dog section. This section has 32 officers and operational dogs, each trained, tested and accredited so that they can be deployed across the British Transport network to ensure the safety of people travelling around the capital.

Because of the training the dogs receive, they will routinely sniff any piece of baggage at stations during random searches. It becomes automatic for the dogs, and the handlers just observe the dogs intently for any sign that the dogs have noticed something that needs to be checked out.

'They have amazing capabilities; their noses are phenomenal,' said Sgt Wanless, who joined BTP after 31 years in the Metropolitan Police, which included 20 years as a dog handler. 'In humans, the olfactory

Wizard … first day on the beach (it's very large!)

Above: Wizard takes a break (from digging?)

Opposite: Wombat with handler Sgt Peter Wanless

glands – responsible for our sense of smell – are the size of a postage stamp. In dogs, they're the size of a handkerchief.' He added: 'The dogs love their work. When they hear certain commands they become switched on, their tails start wagging, and their enthusiasm shoots up.'

The dogs are sourced from a variety of backgrounds – around 20 per cent are donated to the force by the public. Each dog is assessed, and suitable dogs are put on an initial course which lasts eight weeks. They may become operational immediately (like Wombat), but they return every six months for a week-long refresher. During those six months they have to complete a minimum of five days full training. Each time they return for refresher training, the dogs are tested and then re-licensed to show they are up to standard. If they fail, they're taken off operational duties for 30 days, so they can get back up to scratch.

Dogs that have undergone this training are so good – one once detected explosives on an individual who had handled them three days earlier. 'If Wombat enters a room and there are explosives there, I know straight away as his whole demeanour changes,' says Sgt Wanless.

The public is really positive about the work of the teams, and the unit has increased almost seven-fold

SURREY
POLICE

over the past year. 'Ours is a reassurance role; people like to see us out there,' Sgt Wanless explains. 'It also breaks down barriers with the public as people will come and talk to us if they see us with the dogs. It's a job that really enthuses me, because we're able to make a difference,' he added. 'We're committed to helping London's travelling public get about safely.'

Wombat was purchased as an eight-week old yellow puppy. He was a mixture of Golden and Labrador Retrievers and full of the joys of life. He and his brother Wizard, were easy to teach, because they loved to learn new things, but they were difficult to manage due to their irrepressible 'full-on' attitude to everything. As Canine Partners assistance dogs, they need to learn how to stay calm and attentive and be very gentle with the disabled person. Wombat tried very hard to do this, but his natural 'turbo-drive' would win out. He particularly loved hide-and-seek and tugging games, so we had to consider the possibility that Wombat would be happier and less stressed doing a job where those qualities were essential, rather than a nuisance.

Eventually we invited the police to assess him and his brother, and they were snapped up and sent onto training courses immediately. The rest as they say is history. Both dogs were very popular with the Police Dog trainers, due to their outgoing and cheerful natures and desire to keep on working. Wombat is now the 'Face' of British Transport Police and his brother Wizard graduated as a 'Body Dog' – trained to detect human remains and cadavers.

In fact, Wizard showed his 'work ethic' when he was on a refresher training course. On his way to search the field where the remains had been hidden, he stopped and indicated strongly on a patch of ground. The handler knew nothing was buried there, so tried to keep him moving. Wizard froze over this spot, and wouldn't move away, so the handler eventually crouched down to try to work out what the dog had found. Suddenly, he realised what the dog was telling him – four weeks previously, during a different course, some of the pig remains had spilt on that spot. Wizard could still smell it, even though it was a tiny amount and already dried beyond recognition in some

Adult Wizard (and friend) – hey guys, I still believe in Father Christmas!

Opposite: Wizard with handler

particularly hot and dry summer weather. The handler was amazed and of course gave Wizard a full-on game with the ball as a reward, as well as all the enthusiastic praise and hugs he could manage.

This is the sort of quality that is needed in a handler, to bring out the best in a dog. Many handlers and trainers of pet dogs, sport dogs or service dogs do not realise when their dog is telling them something that they don't expect. They just insist that the dog 'obey' and don't take the time to see things from the dog's point of view. But the person who takes the time, who gives the dog credit for thinking 'outside the box' (Wizard was searching long before he got into the field, where the handler planned to actually give him the command to search), and allows the dog to show him/her what the dog knows, will reap the rewards and the unique benefits of this human–animal bond.

Both the instructor, Glenn Winstone and the handler really enjoyed being with Wizard and working together with him. 'What a lovely, lovely dog he is,' remarked Glenn. This comment has nothing to do with whether he looks like a show Labrador, and is all about the dog's personality matched with a handler who can appreciate the dog's good qualities. It is our responsibility too, to place a dog in a situation that suits its personality, temperament and aptitude. This allows that dog to reveal all the wonderful qualities and capacity to co-operate, think as a team and work together with people.

Below: Wizard - 12 months

2006
Holding the Mark
CSI Dog

Chapter FIVE

Forensic Fido – Keela – The Springer Spaniel

When Martin Grime began learning some of the modern and innovative ways to train operational police dogs, he realised the potential for a very specialist way to employ scent detection dogs. Although dogs have recently (see the previous chapter on Wizard and Wombat) been trained to detect human remains that have been buried, no one had thought that dogs might be trained to find something even more specific – droplets of human blood – effectively as 'canine detectives'.

'Don't accept your dog's admiration as conclusive evidence that you are wonderful.'
—Ann Landers

The canine brain has a large part dedicated to analysing and remembering the components of scents. Martin now had the tools (behavioural training techniques and so-called Operant Conditioning principles), to teach a dog to detect microscopic traces of blood. However even he did not know how well some dogs could do this.

Nor did he know whether any dogs would be sufficiently motivated to search for such minute sources of scent. Although he had successfully taught dogs to seek out more obvious smells, such as drugs and human remains, the training of dogs for such a specific thing would be something of an experiment for him. When dogs track humans or other animals, they can follow various clues – such as broken and disturbed ground and vegetation, skin rafts that fall from the moving body, human scent – and footprints or dropped items, which most humans cannot see, let alone smell.

Some humans *can* learn to observe some of the signs that reveal where a person or animal has walked, but a dog can search a wide area for droplets that may not be visible to a person. As Martin says, 'It is like starting a five-year-old child on pure mathematics and then making it more difficult!'

During the research phase of the customer-led project, close consultation by Martin with Mark Harrison, The National Homicide Search Advisor from the National Centre of Policing Excellence, and Jonathan Smith, the National DNA Subject Matter Expert, produced a template for the specific characteristics of the dog to be trained. These included an environmentally safe, socialised and energetic dog that was receptive to behaviour shaping and 'focus' training methods (the 'focus' being considered the most important factor, as the target substance was to be in such small quantities).

Keela searching for clues

Martin obtained a young Springer Spaniel bitch from the breeding programme of the West Midlands Police. Named 'Keela', at 12 weeks old she was introduced to the new training programme. By shaping the behaviour of the puppy during its growth and development, Martin was able to avoid the puppy learning behaviours that would interfere with her ability to perform to the essential high efficiency rating required in this discipline. He was able to reinforce and strengthen her desire to focus on the subject in return for a game with a ball. All the while she was developing the close bond of affection and co-operation with Martin, that would later be essential to her success.

By shaping the behaviour from the beginning, teaching this eager young Springer Spaniel that she would only be rewarded for noticing and alerting him to blood traces, rather than any other part of a human body, Martin was able to utilise Keela's abilities in a very specific way. Using some of the Operant Conditioning principles involved in *Clicker Training*, he was able to shape her responses and her indication

Keela, the CSI spaniel searches a crime scene

to the target scent, despite distractions, or other challenges in the environment.

The effectiveness of this approach meant that Keela became operational at the age of 11 months and began the first of many crime scene investigations immediately. Her first jobs were in Ireland; then she came to England to help solve some high profile cases and eventually her fame spread to the United States, where the FBI called for Martin and Keela to help investigate several murders.

When you watch her in the vehicle, waiting to work, the first impression you get is of a lively, energetic little Spaniel. Then Martin asks her to focus and she becomes very quiet and attentive, eagerly looking towards any potential search sites. When she is calmly told to start searching a vehicle, for example, she becomes an intense, meticulous sniffing machine – going over every part of the car's body, wheels, headlights and the details of door edges, wing mirrors and mud flaps.

Once Martin is satisfied that the exterior of the car is clear, he opens the door and Keela leaps in and begins an ordered sequence of searching, starting at the front of the vehicle, moving to the middle and then to the rear. Martin directs the search pattern, so that he is sure that every section of the interior has been checked, and Keela will choose to go back and double-check any section or object that she has any doubts about. The two work as a team – calm, intense and focussed. From the outside, we can see a perpetually wagging tail and every now and then the sweet little Springer head pop up and check in with Martin, as she busily and tirelessly searches.

If she finds something, she will slow down and start to hone in on a particular area. It might be that there is something under the steering wheel column, or in

Martin Grime with Keela – they travel all over the world to solve difficult crimes

an air vent, or one of the car radio speakers. Sometimes it might be on the seat belt fitting, or under the flooring in the boot. Whatever it is, Martin waits until she tells him exactly where it is. She has to locate the source of the scent. He will not be satisfied until she has clearly held her nose, frozen like a living statue, on a spot for a pre-determined time. She meanwhile is hovering over the spot, willing Martin to come and see and waiting for the marker that tells her he is satisfied and a frantic ball game is on its way as a reward. Only with consistently accurate markers and handler-timing can this high level of accuracy be achieved.

Not only will she search cars and locate such small blood deposits that the forensic science service cannot find with all the technology available, but she will screen hundreds of articles of clothing and locate invisible blood spots even following machine washing in biological washing powder. She will screen crime scenes both in- and out-of-doors and locate blood-stained weapons even after cleaning.

Among many successes, she has located a man's watch that had a tiny spot of blood in the stretch wristband ... after 36 years!

The 'focus' training has a very exciting bi-product. When at home, Martin finds himself responding to Keela's thoughts and body language. He finds himself inexplicably drawn to her cues, as she is to his. This made house-training simple! She is very easy to live with and, as Martin acknowledges, is the most loving and attentive little dog anyone could ever hope to have as a working partner and companion.

Does the perfect dog exist? Maybe, but Keela does have one tiny flaw – one which Martin taught her. He trained her using a treat reward, to 'wait' before jumping into the back of the car. She now refuses to get into the car unless Martin has a treat in his hand. Standing like a statue, she clearly believes that it is always best to look before you leap!

Keela is a beautiful, petite and very fit Springer Spaniel bitch – not only an extremely valuable asset in the detection of evidence to convict murderers, but a loving companion.

What next? Dogs that can analyse DNA?

Top: Cocker Puppy learns to touch for a reward

Bottom: Claire & Tangle, checking traces

2006

Chapter SIX

Guiding and Hearing: Roddy, The Dual Purpose Dog

(by Neil Ewart GDBA UK)

It may surprise you to learn that, unlike many other forms of dog training, the work of the guide dog is not based on any actual instinct. The guide dog cannot work out that its handler is visually impaired and its normal development would not lead it to expect this. So what factors can help make a successful Guide Dog?

'If I have any beliefs about immortality, it is that certain dogs I have known will go to heaven, and very, very few persons.'

—James Thurber

The perfect dog, or human come to that, has never been born. Thus when assessing any animal, you must balance any potential problems against its good points. Temperament is the most important trait that we look for in any potential guide dog. It has to be friendly and sound, as it will be meeting the public in busy urban areas every day of its life. Guide dogs do not have to be too intelligent. The term 'intelligence' is easily misconstrued and means different things to different people. It is more accurate to say we do not want a guide dog to have too much initiative, as its owner cannot see ahead and, therefore, is usually unable to anticipate events.

The question that now arises is, if the training is not based on any instinct, then how does the guide dog learn? The answer is surprisingly simple – by teaching the dog what is required and then consistently give it the right incentives. By effective use of praise and rebuke, the dog will happily do the job even though he does not actually understand why he is performing this way.

Great patience is always required. Like all dog training, the handler must ensure that the dog actually understands a command before it can be corrected for any misdemeanour. Also, it is absolutely vital that the dog is praised effectively when it gets the task right. The dog's desire to please must not be diminished, as this remains the main incentive to work well.

There is nothing new in the concept of selected clients being trained with assistance dogs, when the person has difficulty with their sight and perhaps their hearing too. However, until recently, any dog would only have been specifically trained to meet one of these needs. Any skills later displayed by the dog to give aid for the other disability would have been acquired through experience and subsequent learning.

However there is now an increasing trend for

If you think dogs can't count, try putting three dog biscuits in your pocket and then give him only two of them.
—Phil Pastoret

organisations to work together to produce dogs that are multi-skilled, using the expertise within each organisation.

Angela Hassall lives in the Cheshire area and has a dual-sensory loss, experiencing profound deafness and significant sight loss. Recently Angela became the first person in the UK to train with a dog that acts as both a guide and hearing dog, enabling her to have the benefit and companionship of a dog that performs two important roles: firstly being alerted to important sounds in the house such as the door bell, alarm clock, cooker timer, phone and smoke alarm; and secondly, to be able to get about outdoors safely and comfortably.

When I spoke to Angela recently, she had just moved house and was getting used to all the problems that go with being in a new home; finding places for things, learning new routes and discovering where all the best shops were situated. Angela hasn't always had a hearing or sight impairment, losing her hearing when she was 8 years of age.

This made life difficult at school, as she was frequently told off for not listening properly. She later got married and then got divorced. This was an especially difficult time in her life, coinciding with advice from her GP that she was losing her sight and could in all probability, eventually lose her vision completely. Angela went through a very low period in her life, experiencing depression as she struggled to come to terms with her dual sensory loss.

After contacting Hearing Dogs for the Deaf, she went on to have two successive dogs from them: Darvo and then Buster. Both enabled Angela to be aware of sounds and alerts in her home, as well as providing companionship, but as her vision deteriorated, Angela found outdoor mobility increasingly difficult. Members of the public could be abusive, treating her as if she was drunk, whenever she experienced balance problems or became disorientated.

Eventually Angela became reluctant to go out at all and she contacted her local Rehabilitation Worker and Hearing Dogs to see if there was any option of having a guide dog as well as her current hearing dog, or even to consider one dog performing both roles.

Her request sparked a series of meetings between the two organisations: The Guide Dogs for the Blind Association and Hearing Dogs for Deaf People. A period of collaboration between these charities culminated in Angela receiving Roddy, a Labrador-cross Golden Retriever, the first dual-trained dog in the UK, in 2003.

A significant proportion of Hearing Dogs tend to be small breeds or 'crosses'. However, in order to also act as a guide, a medium sized dog would be required with the initiative to respond to audible signals to alert Angela.

Following more discussions between all parties involved, a couple of likely dogs were identified by guide dog staff based in Bolton. From these, a lovely Labrador x Golden Retriever named Roddy was selected, having been puppy-walked and taken into advanced training as a guide. It was decided to send Roddy to the Hearing Dogs Training Centre for 13 weeks, to be trained in his audible work. This included alerting persons to the sounds of alarm clocks, the telephone, a door bell and, vitally important, a smoke alarm.

Having successfully completed this first part of his training, Tony Cook (Guide Dog Mobility Instructor) spent some time observing this work, before transferring Roddy to Bolton for a further 13 weeks to learn his guiding skills. Naturally it was very important that the guide-dog staff who undertook this were in a position to keep the audible skills up too. To this end, Jackie Boyle from Hearing Dogs would make regular visits to ensure that this was the case. Meanwhile

Right: Angela out and about with Roddy

Roddy took to guiding as easily as he had learnt to acknowledge sounds.

Finally Angela was reunited with Roddy at Hearing Dogs, before spending three weeks learning to work him, with Guide Dogs instructor Lee Stanway.

The result has been a complete success. Angela confirmed to me that she would definitely repeat the exercise and that the key to this has been the very strong and effective co operation between the two charities.

Angela Hassle told Tony Cook that she was teaching Roddy to sound alert to her whilst she was in the bath for when her phone was ringing (she had some residual vision and could just about use the type talk system). She said he was wary of the water so she followed a process of sitting in the bath (fully clothed!) and using a mobile to phone her house type talk phone.

Next she would reward him for putting his paw on the bath side. She would then follow him to the phone and reward. She gradually built up the process, by sitting in the bath in her swimwear and increasing the depth of the water.

Above: Making a difference – Angela and Roddy

Left: WW belt and a 'Goldie' – leaves hands free

This success shows that if trained well, with understanding, enthusiasm and patience, the owner can build upon the dog's existing skills and develop to suit – and it paints an entertaining picture!

Roddy has made a great difference to Angela in many ways. He lets her know when the door bell goes, or the telephone rings and will lead her to the source of the sound. The noise can be a cooker timer or alarm clock, but he will always make contact with her, sitting down in front of her and responding to the question 'What is it?', then leading her to where she needs to be. The only exception to this is if the smoke alarm sounds. In this situation Roddy lies down at her feet and places his paws on her feet. Angela recognises this is the danger alert and takes appropriate action.

As a guide dog, Roddy has enabled Angela to get out more and enjoy shopping and going swimming with the occasional visit to a pub. His training means that he will respond to hand signals with minimal, if any, use of voice. He avoids obstacles, finds objects and stops at kerbs whilst she negotiates the road crossing. There are still times when Angela is unable to assess

Angela and Roddy tackle the road crossing (GDBA)

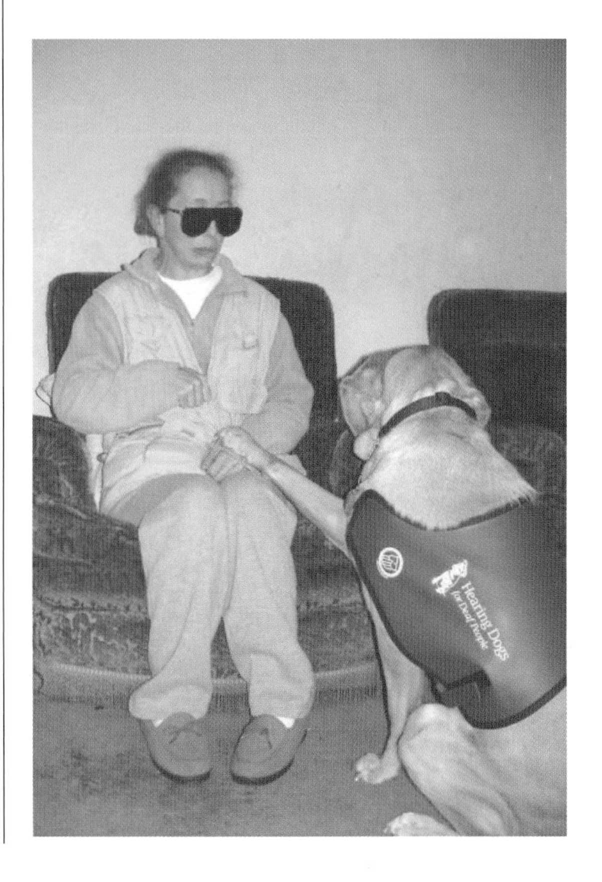

Angela and Roddy get to know each other (GDBA)

whether the crossing is safe but, in such cases, she will always ask for sighted assistance.

Having a dual sensory loss still makes each day a challenge, with her vision fluctuating. At best she can make out some TV programmes, while unable read subtitles. She often makes up the story herself and tries to invent meaning to what is happening, only to find out from her daughter that the residents of Coronation Street are working to a different script! Angela doesn't mind this though and appreciates the days when she can make things out with her remaining vision, as opposed to days when the world is 'blank'.

What next? Angela is currently receiving support from Alison at Deafblind UK to learn 'Moon' and the Deafblind manual. She appreciates the weekly visits and the help in conquering what she describes as a continual uphill battle.

Such battles include the attempts she has made over several years to ask her local Council to provide information in large print. This hasn't happened yet, but Angela remains determined. Being told that someone else could read her mail to her doesn't solve the problem of wanting the same privacy to read as anyone else.

In reply to the comment that she always seems to have a positive outlook on life, Angela says that she always tries to remember 'every day is different but always to keep at it' and recognises that, although there are things she can no longer do – such as knitting – she can get out and enjoy everyday activities, especially one of her favourites, which is shopping!

Having Roddy has helped enormously. Angela realises there are extra responsibilities that come with a dog – hair on the carpet, needing to groom him each day and going to the vets to ensure his health is good. But for her, these are outweighed by the fun and companionship he brings and the assistance to enable a continued degree of independence that would otherwise be considerably more difficult. Many months were required to put Roddy through his training, but ultimately the credit goes to Angela, who worked extremely hard to undergo a rigorous training

Two into one will go!

programme, to form this unique and extraordinary partnership.

Who has benefited? Well of course Angela the recipient who now has a dual-purpose dog. The 'Puppy Walkers' who looked after Roddy during his first 12 months have certainly had their hard work rewarded. Both charities have learned a lot from each other and it is likely that similar projects will occur in the future. Indeed the GDBA and Canine Partners are now working together to dual-accredit a Guide Canine Partner dog named *Cavendish*, for a lady who lectures on ocean cruises – independence indeed.

In conclusion, Angela has been helped to regain much of her own independence, while Roddy has a loving home and a very interesting life! I did ask his opinion but, being the laid back lad he is, he spent most of my visit to Angela fast asleep at my feet!

Chapter SEVEN

Citizen Canine – The Kennel Club 'Good Citizen Scheme'

'Now a year on (from our training course), I cannot believe how much I have done and how much I have gained. My life has changed beyond recognition and while I still have tough times, I know that with the help of "my boy" and the Canine Partners (CP) family I will get through those tough times and be wiser for the experience. Although I remember the course as though it were yesterday, at the moment I wish I were there with you. It's an enriching experience I would love to share again.

I feel I can only really show my thanks to all of you at CP, by always being there for you, whenever you need me. The more people I speak to recently, the more I've been told that it's so obvious how strongly I feel about CP and especially my wonderful Lad in the way I speak about it. It's not hard to do: "a new lease of life" is an understatement of what I feel. I am definitely a "new woman" and I feel I have something to offer to so many people if I can just catch them at the right time. And the nice thing about that is – I never know when that might be!'

Jenny & Free

If you pick up a starving dog and make him prosperous, he will not bite you; that is the principal difference between a dog and a man.

—Mark Twain

Hysterical tabloid press coverage whenever a dog bites a person or a child, has created a rising tide of anxiety about dogs. More and more people are fearful of dogs or actively dislike and distrust them. Fear can prompt a person to behave in extreme or cruel ways towards something; this was seen in the public response to the avalanche of exaggerated reports about the death of a child in Scotland in 1990. The two dogs involved were Rottweilers. Following the publicity, thousands of Rottweilers, both puppies and adults, were destroyed, abandoned, or tortured. Man's Best Friend had become Man's Worst Nightmare.

The mitigating circumstances surrounding the incident were eventually identified as owner ignorance – and taking two young, untrained and poorly socialised

Right: Don't teach puppy to drive!

dogs for granted. The young dogs basically didn't know any better. But this did not stop the tidal wave of negative press and over-reaction. Further reports of American Pit Bulls attacking children, with gruesome descriptions of the difficulty involved in trying to pull the dogs away, triggered The Dangerous Dogs Act 1990 in the UK and Breed Specific legislation in other countries.

This tide of Anti-Dog feeling could only be stemmed by initiatives designed to educate the public on dogs and dog behaviour, so the Kennel Club in the UK set about developing the Canine 'Good Citizen' Scheme. The aim was two-fold: to improve the press for dogs and to educate owners in better ways to own, manage and train their dogs in order to avoid negative incidents. Turning bad press into good dogs is a major success story for the Kennel Club and has triggered other opportunities for dogs to be reported in a more positive way. More television shows featuring dogs being trained or rehabilitated and more events at CRUFTS for which dogs can be trained to compete in events such as *Dancing with Dogs* have gradually improved the public image of dogs.

All the Puppy Parents who volunteer to take one of the Canine Partners puppies for their first year of life will be encouraged to enter the Kennel Club Good Citizen Scheme Puppy Foundation Assessment and try to achieve the certificates that indicate how hard the puppy handler has worked to develop a well behaved and polite puppy.

Every dog owner should aim to achieve at least the Bronze and Silver Certificates and, to that end, there follows an extract from the Kennel club's own information.

Good Citizen Dog Scheme Puppy Foundation Assessment

Those of you who have owned your dog from a puppy will be aware of how important it is to start educating your dog from a young age. Before your puppy settles in to a new environment and starts setting the ground rules, it is vital to provide him or her with an interesting and educational learning programme. This can set the foundations for the future and help you live a happy life with your new family member.

How will courses be conducted?

The *Puppy Foundation Assessment* will be based on the puppy and its owner's attendance at training classes. It is not an award that is conducted on a one-test basis. The thinking behind the Puppy Foundation Assessment course is that puppies learn on a gradual basis, over a period of time. This way a puppy will have time to settle into a new class and gradually build up solid foundations for the future. Upon enrolment onto a course, your puppy will receive an introduction pack including the Puppy Foundation Syllabus, a Puppy Foundation diary and a 'Canine Code'.

How old does my puppy have to be?

The minimum puppy age limit is at the discretion of the training course provider and will be based on the premises and environment used for puppy training. Some dog training clubs may enrol puppies for their course from as young as 10 weeks; other clubs may ask that puppies have completed their second vaccination, whilst other training clubs may like your puppy to be older still. The maximum age for a puppy to enrol will again depend on the individual training club, but will not exceed 12 months old.

How long does it take to complete the course?

Each dog training club or organisation will set their own duration for the courses, e.g. 6–8 weeks, but puppies must attend for a minimum of 4 weekly sessions.

What does my puppy have to do?

As part of any normal dog training process, training the owner is as important as training the puppy; therefore both owners and puppies are assessed. The course includes 12 different exercises and each exercise will be covered as part of each training session. They are:

1. Responsibility and care
2. Cleanliness and identification
3. Attentive response to name
4. Puppy play
5. Socialisation
6. Handling and inspection
7. Puppy recall
8. Basic puppy positions
9. Walking in a controlled manner
10. Stay for approximately 10 seconds
11. Take article away from the puppy
12. Food manners (take a treat without snatching)

Is there an examination at the end of the course?

NO – this programme has been designed to lay the foundations in a puppy's education and therefore assessment will take place over the duration of the course and not on one occasion.

What does my puppy get when he or she passes assessment?

In addition to laying the foundations for a well-behaved dog, puppies who successfully complete the Puppy Foundation Assessment course will be awarded their very own rosette and KC Good Citizen puppy certificate.

Where can I find out about my local course?

Puppy Foundation courses will be run through Kennel Club Registered Dog Training Clubs, Kennel Club Listed Training Clubs, Adult Education Centres and Veterinary Practices approved by The Kennel Club Good Citizen Dog Scheme.

Details of your local course can be found by contacting the GCDS on telephone number 020 7518 1011 or by email on gcds@the-kennel-club.org.uk. **Please include your full name and address when requesting information because packs are posted to you.**

Canine Partners is indebted to the Kennel Club Great Britain, for its superb support, in this book, and day to day.

—Terry Knott,
CEO, Canine Partners

2006

Chapter EIGHT

Bringing Up Baby! So You Want a Puppy

So you want a dog. You really, really want a dog! You want a friend, a companion, a protector, the unconditional love of a furry thing. Before you race out to a breeder or an animal rescue centre, think about what you want a dog for and what kind of a life you will give it.

My goal in life is to be as good a person, as my dog already thinks I am.

—Anon

Think about what it is to be a dog. A dog's job in life is to chew and dig, to bark and run about, to chase things, to play with other dogs, to fight with other dogs, to check p-mail on the trees and gateposts each day, to eat, to drink, to dump smelly heaps on the lawn. He pees, he farts, he keeps an eye out for bitches on heat and he sleeps, preferably somewhere comfortable and high up, such as your bed. A dog has no reason to extend his repertoire beyond these basic activities. He doesn't have to love you, obey you or pay any attention to you whatsoever in order to fulfil his functions as a dog. If you want him to be civilised, you need to make it worth his while. You may expect him to love you because you are his owner and you know how to put food in his bowl. He may not see things quite like that!

Think about this – which person wants the dog the most, but who is actually going to be doing the daily tasks involved in looking after the dog? One partner may want a German Shepherd or a Rottweiler to help them achieve a powerful image, but whoever is at home most of the time is actually the one that the dog will need to work with, understand and develop a rapport with. That person is also responsible for looking after and training the animal, whether or not they wanted a dog in the first place. Whoever takes care of the dog must share the desire to be out in all weathers, dealing with other dogs and have an interest in the learning process involved when a dog finds its place in the human family.

You may want a dog for the kids, but you can't rely on them to look after him. They may beg and claim that they will, but then again, they frequently either lose interest, or they only want to play with the dog or take it with them when they go anywhere. Some children do become very involved in agility training and fun classes, but they are the few, not the many. It is best to presume that they will lose interest, prepare accordingly and be delighted if they do stay involved. The biggest mistake you can make is to get a hyperactive, obsessive dog like a Border Collie or a Springer and treat it like a gerbil, confined for most of the day and hopefully grateful for the occasional ball thrown.

Look carefully at where you live. If it's a flat, you don't need to rule out a dog, provided your daily timetable has room for frequent outings (every two

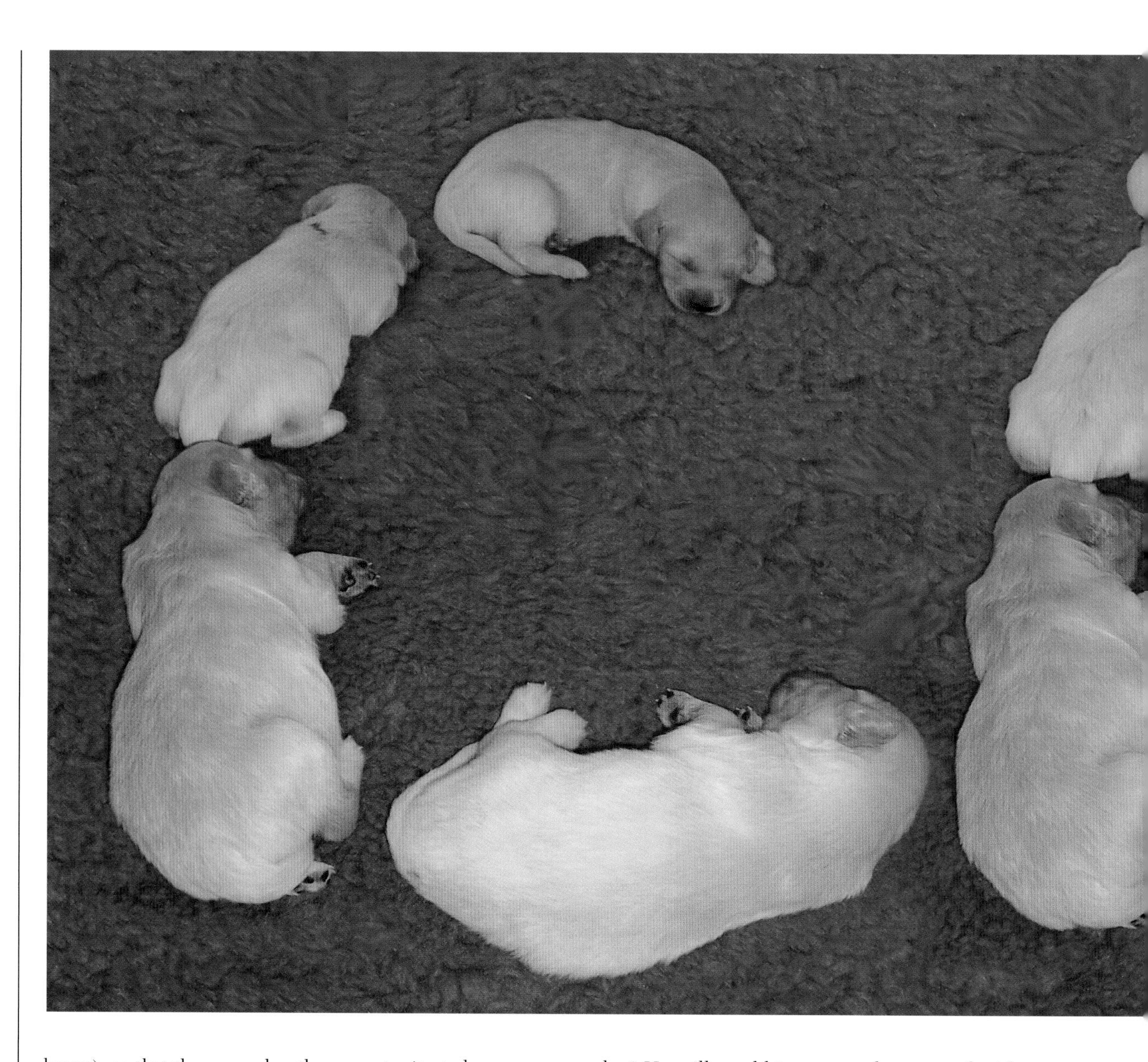

Right: Sleeping future Canine Partners

hours), so that the puppy has the opportunity to learn to toilet in the appropriate place. Remember that a rabbit can be a low maintenance alternative … or a hamster. Both these animals can be clicker trained to come when called and play with you and they have a lower level of need for social interaction, games and company.

Is your garden adequately fenced (and I mean fenced) with wire to the ground and at least five feet high? Even small dogs can leap, scramble and crawl to great heights. Gates need to be to the ground and all holes puppy- or dog-proofed. Is the garden big enough to accommodate the toilet area you will prepare for your dog? He will need his own patch, carpeted with shredded bark, which you will teach him to use so that the rest of the garden remains clean and germ-free. In addition, it pays to remember in the UK that the Fouling of the Land Act means that you are liable if your dog toilets in public and you do not clear it up.

Think about how much time you will need to give the dog. Athletic breeds like Dalmatians, Setters and Springer Spaniels will need a minimum of an hour's exercise – free-running, not once round the block straining at the lead – every day, raining or not. On top of that, you must allocate several 15-minute

training sessions every day. Training time is investment in the dog's life and that is an investment in yours. You will teach him to use his brain – we all know how tiring that can be! – and in that way you can have a dog who doesn't mind sleeping peacefully when you are out and about. When I bred working Rottweilers, I would get up at 5.30 in the morning, go out and lay a track for my dogs, find obstacles for them to practise agility over, go free running, and then they would follow the track and earn some of their breakfast. By the time I left at 7.30 in the morning, they would be left to search for the rest of their breakfast (which I had scattered over the back yard) and then settle down to sleep for the rest of the day. As soon as I got home at night, we would dash out for some fast running and play.

You must set aside time for grooming – how much clearly depends on how large the dog is and how long or curly his coat. Grooming is not a fetish of the show people. Your dog needs to be checked for fleas and ticks and grass seeds which can hook into difficult-to-get-to spots, such as between the feet or inside ears, or cuts and sores which can go unnoticed, or even become infested with maggots under a long, thick or matted coat. With a puppy in the house, you must expect to take him out to his toilet area every 30 minutes or so, throughout the day, especially after eating, playing or waking up.

Now consider the cost. The asking price is only the beginning and currently Labradoodles are selling for over £1,000. Pet insurance is widely promoted, but not necessarily a smart deal for owners; the minimum costs of £10 a month are rising constantly and owners (at the time of writing) are usually expected to pay around the first £40 of every claim. You might find it more effective to make regular payments into your own savings account to cover vets' bills, because you can be certain that you will have to pay them at some point in your dog's life.

He will need a bed (a mat or a basket), a puppy crate for inside the house, and a secure, covered container for travelling. Some form of head control such as a *Newtrix Easyway*, or a Gentle Leader (this is a combined collar and lead with a loop which can fit over the dog's nose and be slipped off to become an ordinary collar) must be introduced immediately, so that the puppy is absolutely used to wearing one. In an emergency, if your dog is in pain and needs to be treated by the vet, you should be able to gently fit a muzzle and your dog can be handled in safety, by you, as well as the vet. Head collars help you walk the puppy and especially a growing young dog, whilst you learn how to teach the dog to walk on a loose lead. You will need a puppy cot for inside the house, along with a waterproof floor protector.

Think about the monthly budget for a dog's daily food (it increases as the dog grows!) plus extra for

I wonder if other dogs think poodles are members of a weird religious cult.
—Rita Rudner

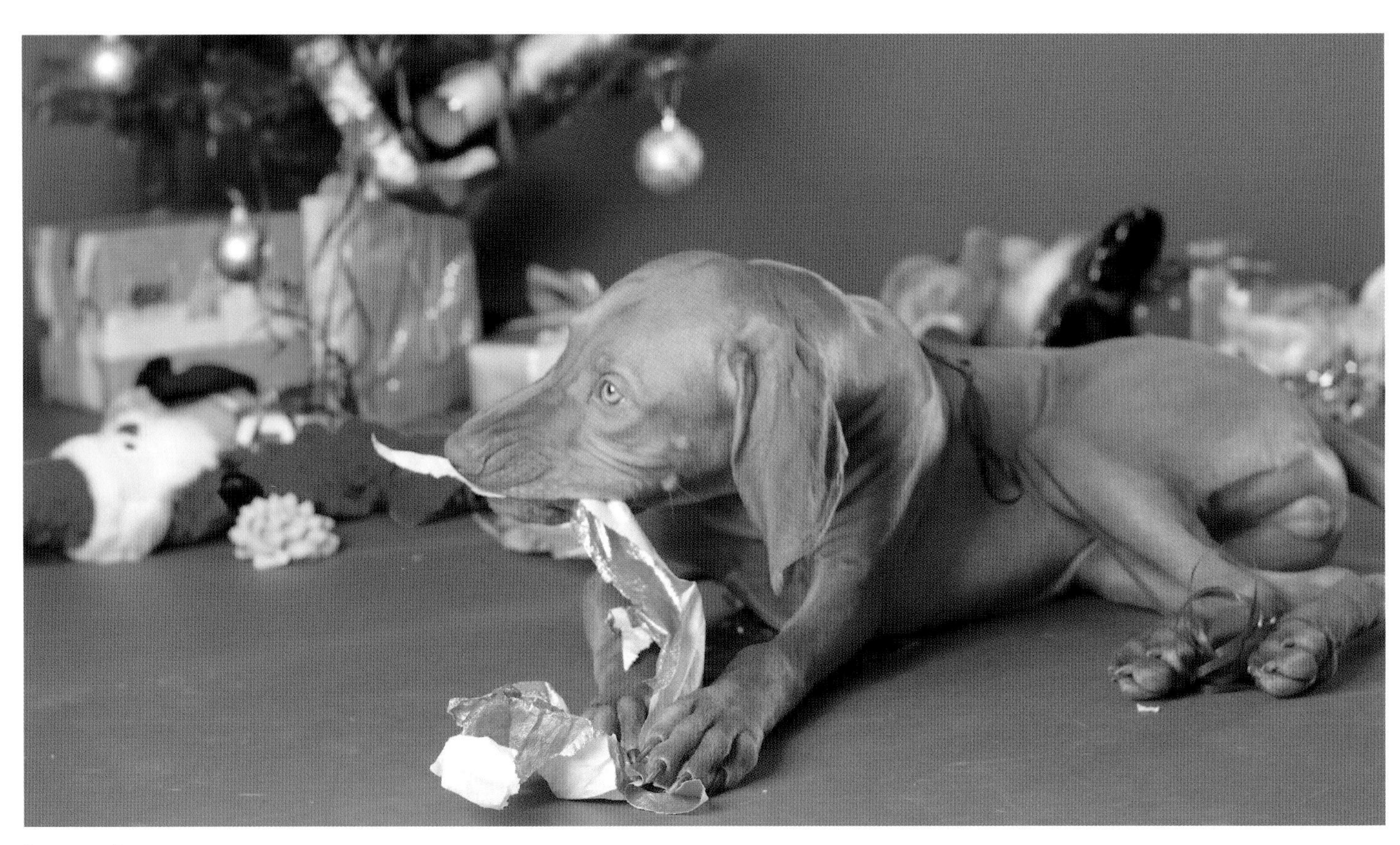

I was sure it was my present!

worming and flea treatments. Add in toys, treats, training DVDs, puppy classes, brushes and combs, and you are looking at a monthly outgoing at time of writing of at least £50. If you don't spend the time and the money, you may be reported for neglect, or your dog will not learn the appropriate way to behave in your home.

Undeterred by all of this, you still really, *really* want a dog?

Think carefully about your preferred breed. Originally each breed was genetically developed to do a specific kind of activity. Then over the years they were bred to win at shows, which means that breeders have tended to concentrate on physical attributes rather than temperamental characteristics. You may like the shape, size and colour of a Terrier but bear in mind that Terriers like to chase things, preferably bite them, and to bark a lot. You may like the shape and the reputation of the German Shepherd. You hope he will be loyal and protective for you and your family. However, there's also a strong probability that he will be reactive, nervous, bark at other dogs and become prey to health problems like chronic wasting of the back legs, or anal sores. The Border Collie is one of the most popular breeds of dog today, thanks to its continuous exposure on television and its reputation for intelligence. Folk memory is crowded with fell-side images of Collies sheep-fetching. However the breed is basically hyperactive – nipping and barking is part of its social inheritance, as well as its obsessive compulsive behaviours.

Yorkshire Terriers, the third most popular breed in Britain, are chosen principally for their cuteness. Their tiny faces and spiky little haircuts make people want to treat them like babies or fashion accessories, but they are Terriers, bred to hunt down vermin. Historically, and consequently what they do best, is to bite – as many people will know to their cost! Training and conditioning can control, but never entirely eliminate, a breed's behavioural characteristics.

Consider whether you want a dog, or an accessory. There is a charming range of backpacks designed to look like a small animal with its arms around your neck on the market. This might be what you are looking for. Just think about it – no pooh to pick up and no waking up in the middle of the night to the sound of whining or barking! There are also CDs that take you through puppy ownership right up to adulthood, and interactive DVDs so you can have all the thrill of dog ownership in the comfort of your living room!

No? You want a real puppy.

Are you certain that the breed you have fallen in love with suits your lifestyle? Then you must decide what qualities are in an individual puppy that would suit you. They are not all the same, any more than brothers and sisters are all the same. Puppies are born different, born individuals, within the breed characteristics. That's why you can get Collies that are afraid of sheep, Terriers that love everybody and Hounds that like to lie by the fire rather than leap over the moors. Many breeders like to be in a position where they can say to a buyer: 'There's one left in the litter. Take it or leave it,' because they don't want to be left with a couple of puppies, growing and costing money, but with no buyers. In this instance the best advice is to leave it and go to another breeder.

When you arrive, you must first of all check the general physical health of the puppies. Do they have bright, clear eyes and cool noses? Coats that are fluffy, clean and shiny? Are they healthily plump, or do they have swollen bellies (a sign of worms)? Does the breath smell clean, the ears smell sweet and fresh and, most importantly, are the poohs (the puppies' excreta) firm and without any blood or slime in them?

A careful breeder will mark and record each puppy when they're first born, so that as they grow and change, you can tell which one is which. A really good breeder will let you visit the litter until the puppies are old enough to be separated from their mother. This gives you a good chance to assess the puppies as they develop rather than falling irrationally in love with one individual on first sight; which is how most people choose the companion that will be living with them for the next 10–15 years!

Above: Zula

My dog chose me

This is a wonderful myth that people believe when they go and look at puppies. They think the one that comes up to them has 'chosen' them. What they don't remember is that the rescue centres and euthanasia appointments are filled with dogs that 'chose' the owner, but were completely unsuitable for the individual's lifestyle or the family's requirements. And by the way, that puppy went up to every other buyer who

Above: Troy

Bottom right: Puppy with keys

Opposite: Puppy with child

came to look because it is very outgoing, confident – even a bit pushy! You need to really know the difference in each puppy and consider what will suit your needs best.

Dogs that are going to be working with disabled people must be gentle, outgoing and cheerful, but they also have to *need* people and that's basically what everybody is looking for in a pet. Most people want a dog that likes people rather than only wanting to get out and play with other dogs. It takes about half an hour to do a simple test, although a full professional assessment on a litter of 10 puppies can be a very long job. Many breeders are not at all keen on buyers doing their own assessment because they simply want you to fall in love with one puppy and give them the money. If they refuse to let you test the puppies, find another breeder – the Kennel Club can help put you in touch. On the other hand, more forward-looking breeders with animal welfare interests at heart, are becoming interested in assessment because it teaches them about their puppies and will help them to breed better dogs.

Tell me who you are

By assessing the litter, you allow each puppy clearly to tell you who they are and what they need from life and a new owner. Look at the whole litter and see how they get on together. Note which ones cower away or move to the back and which ones step up and are happy to sit on your lap. S/he shouldn't be clingy and fearful because that would indicate that s/he is very insecure. Similarly, if the pup barks at you, he is telling you that he is frightened enough to try to scare you – but not frightened enough to run away.

The next thing is to isolate one puppy. Take him or her to somewhere unfamiliar (preferably where the puppy has not been before – like a garage or a gravel path), put him down and hide. Watch his reaction. If he hits the ground running, marches off, and launches his own investigations, he's going to be a very wilful, strong-minded dog. This might be great if you are looking for a dog that you want to compete in trials or train for a working job. He may be terrified at finding himself alone and may scream and yap, but this can also be fine if you live alone, don't go out much and don't have many visitors. Ideally, he will sit there, tentatively start to check out his situation, maybe

Right: Puppies should be alert and curious

back-track a little and gradually gather the confidence to sniff around and investigate.

When you've seen enough, quietly reappear. Don't call the puppy or make kissing noises at him. Just crouch down and clap your hands. Some will run away in terror at the sound. They're the insecure ones and they will need a huge amount of socialisation by you to grow up able to cope with a busy life. Any puppy at that age (between five and nine weeks) that stands back and barks or growls, may grow up with an inclination to bark at or run away from almost anything or everyone. This means that you need to arrange to start going immediately to a behavioural trainer, who can assist this puppy develop more confidence and calmness. Other puppies will simply turn to see what made the noise and get on with what they were doing. These are almost too independent, but will suit people who don't want a needy dog that fawns on them. A highly social puppy will perhaps hesitate for a moment and then come trotting over, lick your hands and be happy to climb into your lap. These pups can adapt to all sorts of lifestyles, families and jobs.

Now you need to gently turn him onto his back and just prevent him from getting up again. If he's kicking and struggling and trying to bite, he is likely to show fiercer resistance later on. If he just lies there, gazing at you and licking your hands, he'll be fine. He trusts people enough to let himself be handled. This tells you how he will behave when a child plays with him (appropriately of course and always under supervision). Next you want to see what he does when you give him an object. Have with you a little piece of

sheepskin on a string (or a strongly made cat toy that dangles, and flicks). Drop it into the puppy's vision and drag it along the ground. He shouldn't want to kill it, nor should he be frightened of it. A cheerful, moderate puppy will pick it up, trot around with it and look very pleased with himself.

At this point, you call to the dog. Unless he's the timid, scared one (which you probably won't want unless you've lost your heart to him), he's got the toy. So he may be trying to kill it or he's trotting around with it. He hears you call and he comes running over and lets you take the toy from him. A more aggressive puppy will growl as if to say: 'Come near me and I'll kill you' or even bite if you try to take the toy. It may be that, with such a highly competitive nature, he would make an excellent working or trialling dog, but whatever he is doing now is exactly what he will want to do to you when he's older. An over-assertive dog will be a difficult household pet and you will need to book in immediately with a behavioural trainer to modify this behaviour. Once you learn the right way to manage this behaviour without punishment or shouting, such a puppy can be a challenging and interesting dog.

By now it's a good idea to test for noise-sensitivity. Take a child's clattering drag toy along and trail it past the puppy. Again he may show terror; he may pounce on it, or he may just take it in his stride. Think about your lifestyle – if you expect the dog to be highly adaptable, cope with all sorts of people and events in your life, then you need a confident, pushy puppy that loves to play very actively with tug and chase toys.

Probably the most important thing to remember is that a puppy will not grow out of his character. He will grow into it. He will get better at what he already does. If he is already growling at you and tearing at your hands, those teeth will get large and extremely powerful. He will also be bigger, stronger, more interested in other dogs and less cute.

There are various Assessment Procedures for selecting puppies that are intended for working homes. When I am testing Beauceron for Ring Sport, or Schutzhund Sport, for example, I will use slightly different tests than if I am testing Rottweilers for Personal Protection Dogs, or Goldiepoos for Assistance Dog work. The qualities I would look for in a Pointer that will work as an explosives-detection dog are different again from those necessary in a dog used for Passive Indication on Illegal Drugs, or Blood.

Above: Observing puppy reaction – does the puppy struggle when held?

The fact remains that each puppy is a mini-adult – individual even at three weeks of age and barely on the earth. Whilst hormones and maturity will certainly modify or change some responses, and life experience will have a huge impact on a puppy, the basic little puppy at that early age will already be showing the tendency to be either bold and forthright, pushy or argumentative, gentle and easygoing, or reactive, timid, noisy, or fearful. The family situation intended for the puppy must take these differences into account. Just as a successful racehorse will not be suitable as a learner pony for a child, so the wrong type of temperament, personality or attitude will make it very difficult for a puppy to fit in easily with your family, or develop the skills to be a Canine Partner, or Fire Accelerant Detection dog.

Rescue me

These are points to watch for closely, if you are considering an adult dog from a rescue centre. Assessment of adult dogs has to be even more rigorous than puppy-testing, for you will never know what abuse the dog has suffered in its previous life, or how he will react to circumstances or events which, unknown to you, raise the ghosts of his past. If anything about the dog bothers you, move on to the next one, no matter how sharply it breaks your heart to do it. Ask to take the dog home with you for a trial stay. Some rescue centres frown on this practice. They are, after all, pushed for space and creatures come in through the door a lot faster than they go out. Some organisations like Battersea Dog and Cat Home, the PDSA and the Dogs' Trust, do offer some basic training or advice to clients. Some encourage would-be owners to take a dog home to try as a temporary guest before signing it over and their *consultants* are happy to give an aftercare service of behavioural advice.

By choosing carefully and thoughtfully, you are giving a wee puppy the best possible chance to live a full, long and happy life, joining in with your family activities, learning wonderful new tasks and skills and possibly one day, even going on to become a *Career Canine.*

Training for life skills

So you have the perfect puppy, chosen with care to complement your personality and your way of life. All you have to do now is civilise it. This puppy has to learn how people think and feel, what they mean when they make noises and pull faces and how to react when grabbed suddenly, or pulled around by a lead.

Puppies which are trained to work with disabled people spend their first year with a volunteer, whose job is to teach them basic civilised behaviour and how to live alongside human beings – at all times. That means that they must be able to cope with heavy traffic, trains, buses, football games, high-street shopping, post offices, banks, rock concerts, road-works, other dogs, cats or whatever. Each must be a dog of the world. At the same time, never, ever forget that he doesn't have to do anything except be a dog. In his classic study, *Understanding Your Dog*, the Austrian behaviourist, Eberhard Trumler describes the development of his 60-odd specimens, a hybrid collection of Dingoes, Alsatians and dogs of unidentified origin, many of them interbred in Trumler's research compounds. He experimented with different patterns of rearing puppies, on one occasion taking his Alsatian puppy Rana away from her mother at the age of eight weeks and giving her into the sole charge of her father, Sascha. Trumler says: 'The father joined in all Rana's games, taught her other ones, and tolerated all her pranks. Now that Rana is full-grown, it is impossible to play with her; nor can one teach her anything. It is hopeless. At the first contact she cringes and tucks in her tail. We get the same reaction from all puppies reared by the father(s). Such puppies cannot comprehend that man is kind and a being that one can play and work with.'

Right: Malcolm & Didi

Above: Restrain puppy to test reaction

So unless at this very early age you concentrate on accustoming your puppy to life with humans – and with other dogs – you will have trouble later on. Just like children, a puppy reaches an age when his little brain can absorb unlimited experiences and he can learn how to deal with them. Of course he needs to feel safe with you so that he can handle the unexpected, but once he has learned how to respond to the shocks and surprises that life throws at him, he will be able to grow into a calm, steady, unflappable adult. Here is where we have a problem because the pharmaceutical and veterinary industries have conditioned us, the dog-owners, into believing that a puppy should live a cloistered existence until his 14th week, because unless we fill him full of chemicals and keep him away from the contagion of other dogs until the chemicals have worked their magic, he will not live to see his 14th week. He will fall prey to parvovirus, leptospirosis, distemper, kennel cough or tetanus and a dozen other imagined ills.

These are the diseases against which standard vaccinations offer some protection. This presents a very real dilemma, since the optimum period for socialising a puppy is between 3–12 weeks. After that the patterns of his responses are pretty much fixed. He can learn new activities, but his internal landscape is drawn and painted and will remain his point of reference for the rest of his life. If the landscape is a desert, he will be unable to make sense of anything in the everyday world. Everything there will represent a threat and you will find yourself in charge of a nervous, growling, lunging, barking dog. The question for you, his guardian and keeper, is whether you put his body or his mind at risk in this sensitive period of development. It is useful to remember that most diseases which affect a dog are airborne and that you can walk them into the house without taking the puppy out to find them. Isolation, therefore, is no guarantee that the puppy is not exposed to germs.

It is also a good idea to find out whether your puppy actually needs immunisation. Most dogs retain a high immunity for years without the aid of vaccinations and boosters. You might need to be rather assertive with your vet, who is likely to be persuaded

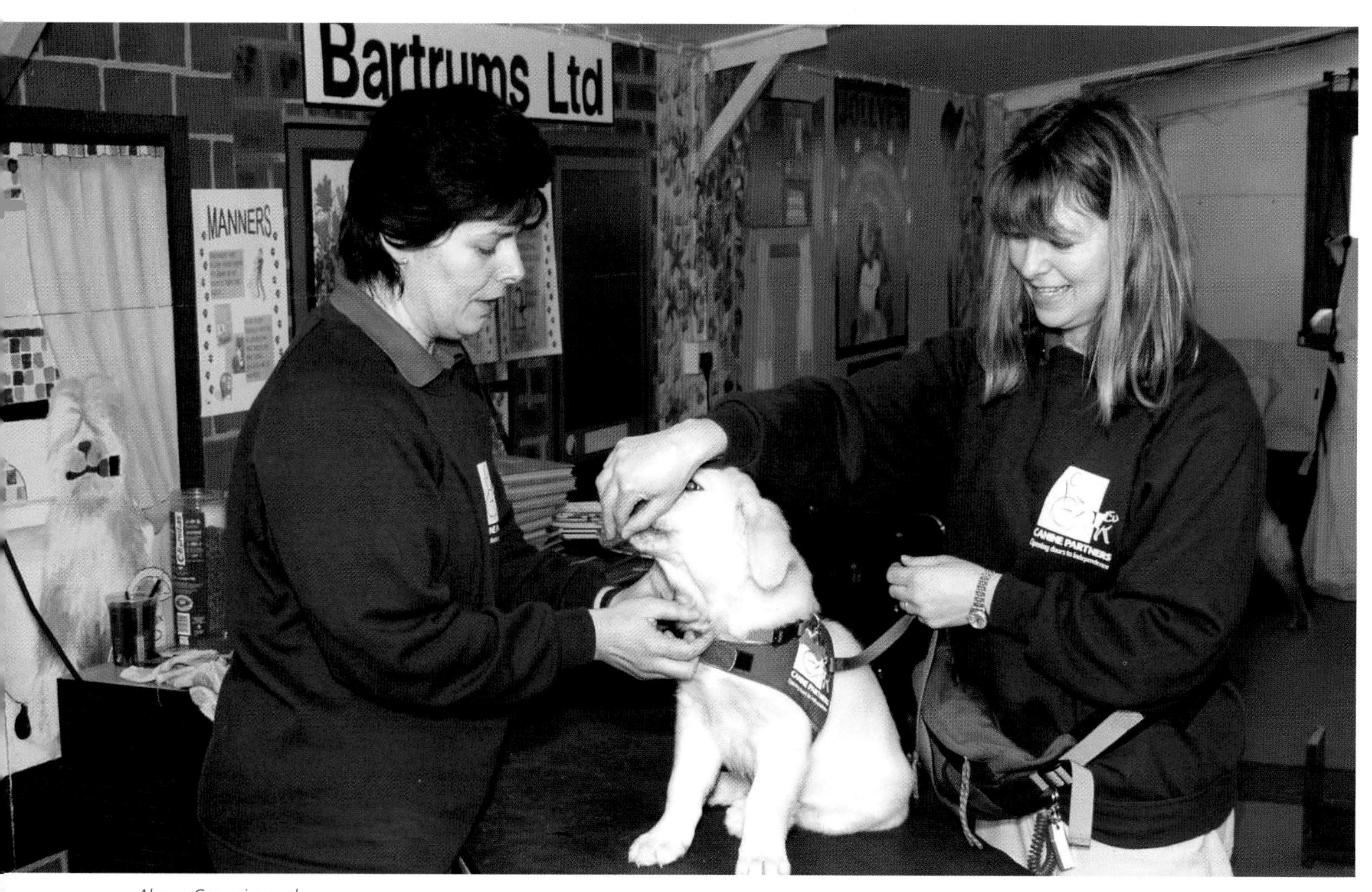

Above: Grooming and weighing puppy. Sandra and Di in the old Training Centre at Petersfield.

by the pharmaceutical manufacturers that their products are irreplaceable life-preservers, but you could suggest that your puppy be titre-tested. This is a blood test which reveals the dog's levels of immunity and indicates for vaccination only if it shows that he needs additional protection – the principle of 'If it ain't broke, don't fix it'. It's a system which is gaining ground in America, but few vets in this country are geared up to do the test in the way that they will routinely administer vaccinations.

Now, then, your puppy is ready to be socialised.

A puppy of the world

Taking the puppy out into the world is not unlike expeditions with young children and all the accompanying paraphernalia that their outings involve. You will need a rucksack, your clicker, a range of treats and toys for the puppy. Put the puppy in the rucksack and all the other ingredients in a convenient carrier and get out into the hurly burly. Limit the outings to half an hour or less in the first few days, but make sure that, over the first couple of weeks, the puppy experiences as many different circumstances and surroundings as you will expect him to handle in later life. He needs to become accustomed to people with loud voices, children screaming, prams, trains, buses, shops, air brakes on lorries, pedestrian crossings, emergency vehicles, tractors, even fireworks.

Watch his every reaction while you still have him in the rucksack. He will feel safe here, next to you but will be watching life going on around him. If he takes an interest in something new to him and just accepts

it without getting excited, click/treat. If something – a lorry screeching to a halt, a siren or some sudden event – upsets him or makes him nervous, stroke him calmly but don't click. You will have assessed the medical risks of setting him down in places frequented by other dogs and made your own decision about how to proceed. You may decide that you would prefer to keep him isolated until his jabs have taken, but it will help him to cope with the world outside if he sees some of it, even from the protection of a carrying-bag, in this receptive period of youth. If he's a big breed, you may find his bulk rather more than you can handle as he approaches his 12th week. At home you can accustom him to strange and scary noises with sound-effect tapes – fireworks and bird-scarers – played at a low level while he is safely in his crate or lying on his mat.

The main point here is that you are moderating the dog's reactions. You avoid click/treating a bullish, feisty puppy for barking at new sights and sounds, and similarly you avoid click/treating a nervous, shy dog for cowering away from them. You are changing the dog's perceptions so that strange moving objects, loud noises, brightly-coloured flapping things, or whatever he is being introduced to, are both interesting and something that he can handle. He feels neither threatened nor carried away with enthusiasm for them.

Some puppies may be startled and then fearful of a post office box, or something else in the street that you take for granted. Socialising a puppy can attract nervous glances from passers-by, who may not appreciate the processes at work, but so long as you remember that you are conditioning the dog to live peaceably alongside the human race, you can probably overcome your own self-consciousness. It's a full day's work for the owner. When the postman arrives in the morning, you are there with the click/treat. The mail has come through the door and this is a great event which you and the puppy celebrate together. It's also a risky moment, for puppies have been known to eat cheques and bills indiscriminately, so it's important to get there first and click as soon as the puppy sees the mail, because you will redirect the puppy onto the treat and away from the post.

Similarly the noisy garbage truck, visitors, children or friends coming for dinner, all need to be greeted as if they are fun things. Intervene if your visitors try to lean over the puppy, adorable as he is, making baby noises, because puppy will try to jump up and either lick the face, or bark or try to push the person away by behaving excitedly and frantically. Get a friend to help you practise this behaviour by arriving, standing still and waiting until the puppy is calm, before just treating and then turning and going outside again. Repeating this action 10 times in 20 minutes will very quickly teach your puppy that people knocking on the door is a cue to hurry into a calm, preferably lying down position, because this is the quickest way to (a) get treats and (b) not have to say 'hello' to people and feel slightly stressed.

Below: Ow! Puppy must learn a gentle mouth

Right: Let me see too!

Your puppy needs to have permission to greet people. Puppies need practice but are, on the whole, quick to learn. They are, at this period of their lives, programmed to accept new relationships and you must make the most of the short time span available. A dog can absorb and deal with his social experiences up to the age of about 14 weeks. After that, he is pretty much set in his ways and the unfamiliar is either frightening or threatening. Of course, if you have accustomed him to experiment and cope with new situations, he will continue throughout his life to be open and enquiring and willing to participate in social adventures.

The new puppy

You have chosen your puppy, prepared your house and garden for him and done your own clicker homework. You collect him from the breeder or the rescue home (if rescue home, you've had a day with him to make sure you get on). You or the children want to cuddle him on your lap while you take him home. He's the best new toy you've ever had. Actually, what he needs

is a nice, secure puppy crate, or even better a carrying case in which to travel, from where he can feel protected because it is enclosed, but he can still see what is going on through the door. If he is in the crate, he is not climbing over the seats, getting under the driver's feet or doing something potentially dangerous or unpredictable.

Already he is adapting to a life quite different from the one he has known for his first six weeks and he has more than enough of the unfamiliar to assimilate without strange new people arguing over who is going to look after him. He does not, as yet, love you as much as you love him. If you have far to travel, it is worth giving him a homoeopathic car sickness remedy (see The British Association of Homoeopathic Veterinary Surgeons, www.bahvs.com). He is most unlikely to have been in a car before and he may find it both uncomfortable and frightening. (Actually some very good breeders are now making sure that the puppies are taken out on regular car trips before they go to their new homes.) Keep him as calm as possible, by yourself staying calm and relaxed. Don't pat him when he is barking. Pat him when he is quiet and keep it to a minimum for his reassurance. Some puppies see a huge hand bearing down on their head as a thing of horror when they are already stressed in a strange new situation.

The moment you get home, take the puppy to his toilet area and wait with him. As soon as he squats, whatever he does, click him and give him a No 1 treat and heaps of praise. The click will certainly surprise him but the treat, following instantly, will begin to establish it in his mind as a marker of something significant. If he has simply had a pee and you think there might be more to follow, wait with him a little longer. If you get a result, click/treat again. If nothing happens, put him on his Gentle Leader, take him into the house and give him another 20 minutes before you take him back to the toilet area. For his first few days, the puppy will need to relieve himself every 20 minutes or so.

This is not the drudge it might first appear to be. It's a godsend because it presents an opportunity to make the click/treat regime truly meaningful. It accustoms the puppy to a strange, sharp sound which might have alarmed him to start with and teaches him that it is worth listening for. It also makes for a clean house, which is the first most important part of training for any dog-owner. You take him out to his toilet area every 20 minutes, so that you are giving him every opportunity to get it right. Do not leave him alone in a separate room in the house. Keep him reasonably near you in one room with his mat or basket and be alert to what he is doing. When he needs his toilet area, he gets very little warning; he will start to sniff and circle the ground at which point you whisk him out to the garden and wait until he's finished. Click/treat exuberantly. This is the positive, proactive way to educate a puppy.

If the worst comes to the worst, you miss all his cues and there's a mess on the floor, there is absolutely nothing you can do about it except clear it up, discreetly, with the puppy in his crate where he cannot see you. Use a deodorising spray or powder which kills the smell of urine (not bleach or ammonia which do not fool the canine nose) and the puppy will not run away with the idea that he has created an acceptable

Below: Posh toilet area

Above: Plain toilet area

lavatory spot. Extravagant punishment is counter-productive. It teaches the puppy to defecate where you can't see him do it and does nothing to help him learn that his loo in the garden is where he should be going. Be prepared for perhaps a week of broken nights – maybe only 2–3 if you are both attentive and lucky. You cannot expect the puppy to sleep peacefully in the kitchen at this stage of his life – for 6–7 weeks he has slept up against his mother or in a pile of his brothers and sisters. He cannot cope with sleeping alone yet. When you go to bed, put him in a box, a basket or his crate, together with a rug and a chew, or a toy – something to gnaw on – in the bedroom. It does, for now, have to be the bedroom.

Turn out the light, give him a stroke and say gently: GO TO SLEEP. If he whimpers, ignore him. If he gets loud, touch his head, say the words again so that, although he can't see you, he knows you are still in the room. He may whimper some more but he will soon see that he achieves nothing by it and he will go to sleep. Do not wake him up for his toilet routine. At three or four or five o'clock he is guaranteed to need his lavatory and he will whimper and yelp and scream because puppies will not soil their own nests. Pick him up, run him down to his garden area, where you use your chosen cue-word for toileting, wait with him until he has finished, click/treat profusely then take him back to his bed with a big cuddle and a new chew to settle him for the rest of the night. At this stage of their lives, puppies do a lot of sleeping but when they're awake, they require continuous entertainment. This is when you start clicking. The click is always followed by a high-value treat, the chicken, lamb or liver, to assure the puppy that a click is something very important. You will have already worked out how much food your puppy needs each day and bear in mind that in the wild, he would be accustomed to tear at his meat and gnaw at bones. Bones often have a dramatic effect on domestic puppies' digestion but a cabbage stem or a carrot to chew on can be very soothing to the sore gums caused by teething around this age. Given to him after his main meal, the chewing will help his digestive system and help prevent Canine Bloat.

This is a good time to start clicking the puppy for allowing his mouth and face to be handled. Lift his lips with your fingers, click/treat. Lift the lips again, look over his teeth and gums, click/treat. Go over the same routine with his ears. The dog learns not to go for your face and hands while you are examining him which you will need to do all his life in the search for ticks, fleas, grass-seeds and gum disorders. He will feel safe while his mouth is being handled and he will not have to defend himself by barking. It will also steady him during visits to the vet, which is important for all dogs but especially for the hunting breeds and Terriers which are likely to develop into very strong-minded adult individuals.

The key to clicker-training is to treat the entire session as a game. Discard any preconceptions you may have about the master–slave relationship between you and your puppy. Certainly you are in control of the relationship but, within that framework, you are educating a puppy to perform tasks for you because he wants to, not because he is scared. Unquestionably the way to make him want to work with you is to ensure that he is having a good time, not submitting reluctantly to your onerous demands. A classical trainer might well feel that to praise and reward a puppy for

wagging his tail was a pointless exercise because a puppy will wag his tail anyway. Click/treat a puppy when he wags his tail and you are 'telling' him that wagging his tail and being a cheerful little animal is a nice way to be and that is how you want him.

Do not expect perfection at this stage. Anatomically your puppy is not yet developed enough perhaps even to sit without rolling over, but this is also worth click/treating because you will eventually want him to roll on his back to order (it's a useful submissive posture and it might be essential for veterinary examination) and you have a golden opportunity to begin shaping that behaviour. If there is a rule of thumb at this point in the training, it is: don't click if the puppy is doing something you don't want him to do. Otherwise, click everything. Every movement he makes is on track to an activity you will want him to perform when he is older. For example, puppies of this age have been accustomed to drink from the teat while their mother is standing up. They use one paw to press against the teat and stimulate the milk-gland. They are therefore perfectly able to support themselves on three legs with one paw lifted – the classic shake-hands posture which is valuable beyond price when it comes to greeting visitors to the house. Not only is it almost unspeakably cute, it is a posture which by definition prevents the puppy from jumping up to lick the visitor's face. This kind of behaviour in an adult dog is likely to knock a person off their feet which is normally regarded as less than desirable.

Above: Xyla

Below: Puppies kissing – AH!

2003

Chapter NINE

Select A Breed – All You Ever Wanted To Know

(or Pick a Pup – Nature, Nurture and the Face that Fits)

Canine Learning is a concept that is not very familiar to people. Everyone talks about training the dog to 'do' something, but they rarely talk about how a dog might best learn something. Initial puppy training forms the foundation for all kinds of activities – whether it is Assistance dog work, Police operations, search and rescue, tracking and agility work or just being a wonderful and responsive family companion. But, life is stressful, and puppies, like us, react differently to stress in all its forms. Buying a Border Collie to leave in a flat all day, is as stressful to a dog as you being in a dead-end job with no chance for you to express the skills, talents, and drive that you know you have.

So this needs to be taken into account when we want to buy and train a dog; we can make a more informed decision about what breed or type of dog might be the most suitable.

'A dog teaches a boy fidelity, perseverance and to turn around three times before lying down.'
—Robert Benchley

Puppies begin learning as soon as they are born. They have to, in order to survive their first few weeks of life. However, their nervous system is fairly basic until about three weeks of age, when the eyes begin functioning better, and information about the world begins to flood into the puppy. So, like me, they are basically thinking about food.

Life stages – *'A need-to-know basis'*

Puppies go through various stages in their development and throughout their lives. From the age of three weeks, up to four months an enormous amount of information must be taken in about the environment, because the puppy needs to quickly understand what things are: 'An all new, improved, Expanda-brain' comes as standard issue. They need to know family members, and the correct way to interact with other dogs without getting into trouble. They need to then learn about the world around them in order to avoid danger, play nicely with brothers and sisters, eat, drink, and develop physical coordination, control and skills to get on in life.

For this reason, the brainwaves of a puppy are operating at a faster frequency than they will after the puppy matures. Puppies are like blotting paper, absorbing a huge amount of knowledge about life and their surroundings, without reserve. They then go through a phase of processing and storing that information, so that they know how to react as they grow up. Whether you are aware of it or not, puppies are learning by association, by observation, by trial and error and by experimenting, each day. They are mini-surveillance systems – both with the breeder and once they are placed with the new owner, the puppy is trying to make sense of the world. They are not ignorant or stupid, or unable to be taught, as so many authorities have stated in the past. It is a basic survival skill to be able to learn, and puppies have that skill in bucket loads!

Life learning

Puppies learn by doing – whether that is chewing or rolling over, or biting, barking, scratching, digging, sniffing, tasting, eating and any of the other activities that they get up to. This is life learning – learning from experiences. This tells them how they should respond in the future to new or unexpected events or things. The puppy also learns how to influence others in the environment, and to interact in the world the right way, to avoid trouble. This is why it is essential that puppies experience the traffic, noises, sights and smells of a busy urban environment, from the age of three weeks, whilst they are still young and eager to learn. If you leave this socialisation until three to four months of age, it may be too late.

Since puppies are social beings, and survive by adapting to a group structure with a hierarchy and rules of behaviour, greeting behaviour is a basic skill that a puppy must learn. Whilst dogs are not wolves, and indeed, are more like scavengers in their social activities, they are still hardwired to react from a doggy point of view to events around them. So, we can observe behaviour in related species to get some idea of what dogs learn and when they learn it.

Left: Kermit
Opposite: Goldie

CANINE
PARTNERS
SUPPORTED BY
PURINA

Canine Friend Gaia

Meet and greet – or die

All puppies have to learn the correct way to say 'hello' to new dogs – no jumping up on them, no shouting, no biting of tails or testicles, and certainly no stealing food from big dogs.

The other lesson a puppy needs to learn is how to regulate the power of its bite. By giving puppies little pointy sharp teeth, nature ensures that even the slightest bite will hurt. By experiencing this itself, and experiencing the screams and growls of puppies on the receiving end, a puppy learns to moderate the way in which the jaw closes, in every situation. In the same way, we teach a puppy, from three weeks of age, that human skin is fragile and 'gently does it' every time. If the biting gets too sharp, the game stops.

Feet first

In the same way, a puppy learns to paw at something to see if it moves, or touch something to check it out, or try to play with it, or even just to decide whether it is dangerous or not. Feet are great for getting under the ground, or into a pile of leaves, or for pulling something towards a puppy.

Puppies can learn to use their paws to help us when they are older. We can make a special digging pit in the garden, and teach the puppy to always go there for a dig, because treasures have been buried there – one day some dog treats, another day a bone, or a tuggy, or some frozen carrots, or some tuna oil and bread. This keeps puppy off the other parts of the garden.

Use it or lose it!

We can set up similar learning situations from the age of three weeks (breeders take note!) and teach the puppy about OUR world. We can teach the puppy (or rather teach the puppy how to teach itself) how to survive in a people-oriented world, in a family environment, in a street and park, or anywhere else the puppy may live as an adult. If you leave a puppy without this stimulation from the age of three weeks, they will not properly develop those parts of the brain that control the experiential learning ability. In other words, the puppy will never be as smart or as confident, and adaptable, as its genetic potential would allow it.

Puppy professors

By teaching component behaviours, and then allowing the puppy to experiment with those behaviours, Canine Partners develop the puppy's ability not only to learn and problem solve, but also the ability to deal comfortably with stress and conflict.

It is a safety consideration that a puppy must be able to cope with stress without becoming panicked or aggressive. Also that the puppy does not quickly cross the threshold of frustration and become aggressive or unpredictable. Working dogs – especially General Purpose Police dogs – are stressed on the job intermittently. Assistance dogs are stressed whilst working in public because they are not allowed to just relax and be a dog. We need to teach puppies how to cope with stress, and also select the right job to suit a puppy's ability to deal with challenges.

But, let's not forget, it is actually intensely rewarding for puppies to learn how to interact with people and the objects and situations in the world, because they will become more relaxed and confident. We all feel happier if we know what's going on and what we can do about it if we want to change things! If we can learn to 'read' our puppy or dog, we can choose the breed and most appropriate training approach, home, family and job to allow that puppy to achieve a rewarding and exciting life, communicating easily with humans and other dogs alike.

What do we mean by 'read' your dog?

How do you know what your dog is saying to you? Can you tell what your dog needs at any time? You should know the difference between when your dog needs the toilet, is tired, anxious, stressed, confused, or frustrated, and any other signs your dog gives you about how he/she is feeling. It may seem difficult at first, because so many of the signs aren't so obvious, but you will be surprised how quickly your ability to do this will develop if you practise.

Many people don't know what their dog is trying to tell them, and they may then have problem with misunderstood or difficult 'problem' dogs. We owe it to our dogs to learn what they are trying to tell us at all times. Also, we should to be able to respond appropriately, and to remove or protect our dog from situations he/she cannot cope with. You also need to be able to ensure your dog's needs are met – this is essential for your dog's welfare and physical well-being, and for any working dog to be able to do their job properly. Dogs are social creatures – they need to be with others. If they can't be with other dogs, then they need an alternative, and that is usually you and your family.

Left: Didi - Goldiepoo

Top: Play time – frizbees make an ideal chase and fetch toy!

Bottom: Goldie on pool edge; fish for supper

Sometimes I just sits

I want that one!

'I bought him to match the furniture, but I don't want him sitting on it.' If you are choosing a dog, and you are looking at particular breeds, or mixed breeds, colour and cuteness may seem like the way to decide. But the sad truth is, the way your lifestyle might impact on the dog, and what your responsibilities as an owner will be –depending upon which breed or type of dog you choose is actually far more important.

Canine good citizens

One way to help your puppy develop into a responsible adult is to book you and your puppy into the Kennel Club's Canine Good Citizen Scheme, and earn your Bronze, Silver and Gold Certificates. Also, find an Instructor who has passed the Kennel Club's Trainer Accreditation Scheme. This was covered in Chapter 7.

What do they do?

Before you rush to buy, firstly research the original purpose of the breed, since this will give you a clue as to how the dog is likely to behave in daily life. Dogs bred to fight, will be inclined to do so. Dogs bred to hunt, will love hunting. Dogs bred to run for hours will go crazy if they don't get that level of exercise daily. When you buy a particular breed, and hope that it will adapt to your lifestyle (which probably doesn't include boar-hunting, bear-baiting, ratting, or sheep-herding in the Scottish Highlands), then you need to modify your situation to channel the dog's inbuilt drives to behave in a certain way. One of the major stressors of modern dogs is being left alone all day in a home, unable to do the things that are their genetic heritage.

Stress – the good, the bad and the ugly

Stress is essential for you or your dog to learn anything. Without a challenge, or a goal, or that rush of excitement, anticipation, or performance nerves, it is difficult for you to test your limits, or extend yourself. If a dog was not excited at the sight of a rabbit bolting off over the fields, it would be very difficult to teach the dog to chase and hunt. And if dogs didn't want to chase and hunt, it would be even harder to teach them to be Police dogs, or detect explosives or cancer cells or herd sheep.

So stress is good for you and your dog. But you can have too much of a good thing, so when there is too much stress, the body cannot recover quickly enough. This means that the system gets overloaded, and begins to break down. In fact, stress-related disease and injury is now common in the workplace and in the performance field. Dogs can be stressed to the point where their bodies begin to malfunction, sending signals that cause problems in the way that the dogs function or respond to their situation.

The sweet dog that 'loves people' suddenly starts growling at visitors or family friends; the playful dog that now cannot seem to relax and settle down; the Police dog that bites the handler, or cannot be called off the suspect; the assistance dog that develops skin problems, and beings to chew its feet or tail. All of these dogs are exhibiting signs of possible stress. Unless you deal with the cause of the stress, you cannot solve the behaviour problems by punishing the dog – in fact you will probably make it worse.

A sign of the times

Here are some of the general signs your dog might use to try to tell you how he is feeling. However, all dogs are different so you need to get to know your own dog.

Fear, anxiety, stress

Some signs are obvious – like the signs that a dog is feeling fearful or anxious:

- Avoidance – physically moving away from the scary thing, not looking at, or not facing it.
- Attempting to bolt or lunging (away from scary thing)
- Aggression – depending on a dog's previous experience and available options, he/she may try to use aggression to make the scary thing go away. This can include growling, barking, bared teeth and lunging towards it.
- Raised hackles – this is a line of raised hair which can begin on the top of the head and continue to the tip of the tail. However, you can usually see raised hackles around the top of the shoulders. Dogs do this to make themselves appear bigger.

Most people see a dog growling and barking, and interpret this as a dangerously aggressive dog. But the dog is really trying to put distance or space between itself and the scary thing – either by running or creeping away, if possible, or if on the lead or tied up, trying to scare the thing away by shouting a warning. This is not behaviour that should be punished. Actually, we need to change the association, so that the scary thing means good things for the dog.

Some signs are less obvious and very likely to be confused with other things:

- 'Stress signs' – can include yawning, panting, licking, sniffing, scratching (particularly around collar/neck area), licking/chewing self. For more info refer to '*Calming Signals*' books and videos by Turid Rugaas.
- Fixating – some dogs will stare at a scary thing and refuse to look away. Their pupils will also dilate in order for them to take in as much information as possible. Their weight distribution is likely to be over their hind quarters (they will appear to be leaning back) in order to make a quick getaway!
- Pacing – cannot settle down, or relax, salivating.

If the dog is out in public, firstly, identify the source. Is it due to a specific object, or a person? Or is it an unfamiliar noise? Is the general environmental surroundings such as crowded train station, noisy event or even unknown, strong smells scaring the dog? Does your dog pull away when being handled around the face or head? Does your dog pant or whine when a dog, stranger or a child approaches?

Next, either take the dog away or step between the dog and the stressful thing. Reward the dog for all behaviour that is not aggressive. If any of this behaviour occurs during a training session, especially barking, jumping, growling, and spinning or pacing, the dog is possibly frustrated or confused. Perhaps you are not clear in the training, or the dog is not getting enough reward to keep trying, or your timing is poor. The dog feels intense irritation and tried to demand that you improve! So you might see any of the following:

- Barking
- 'Mischievous' behaviours – such as chewing, stealing objects (e.g. remote control!)

Labradoodles assorted!
Gaia, Quest and friend

- Whining/whinging
- Depression – a long-term symptom of boredom or learned helplessness. Learned helplessness can also be seen typically in dogs that have been trained with electric shocks. They make no attempt to get away from something that is unpleasant or painful, and people refer to them as 'shut down'.

Dogs get frustrated and anxious, when left alone every day. They prefer to live with others, and get very distressed if forced to live alone. If this is the case you need to examine your relationship, looking at the interactions between you both. Arrange things so that your dog has something to think about and do throughout the time you are away from the house. Stuffed and frozen Kongs, or marrow bones, or other rubber chew toys can be hidden for the dog to find. Or you can make a digging pit in the garden and hide treats, toys, pieces of vegetable, bones etc in the pit daily.

Also, an event that you think of as 'fun' for the dog, such as a visiting dog that plays enthusiastically, or a trip to the local pub for lunch, is stressful for many dogs. They will need a couple of days to recover, so you must make sure that the dog is given the chance to relax and just rest for at least a day after such an event. If your dog never gets enough opportunity to relax, rest and recover, then you will start to see the strange behaviours that I mentioned opposite.

Choosing the right dog – the stress factor

Stress can be great or very undesirable. New research into the effects of negative stress on puppies and dogs has indicated that many so-called 'behaviour problems' may be an indication that an otherwise healthy dog is experiencing stress at levels which can no longer be tolerated. Whilst a small amount of stress is essential for developing and maintaining a dog's immune system and ability to cope with and recover quickly from stressful events, the effects of long-term stress are potentially damaging to a dog. You don't want your dog becoming a 'Stresshead'!

Because dogs were bred to react in specific ways in order to do their jobs properly, they also react differently to stress. What is stressful for one puppy may be just what another puppy needs, depending upon the breed as well as the individual.

It is no coincidence that many of the very active working roles for dogs that involve close cooperation with people tend to be filled by dogs from the Gundog, Herding, and Working or Utility breeds (see Appendix). These breeds were developed by selecting for breeding only those animals that were easy to manage by people and highly focused on the specific target – the sheep, the cattle, the goats, or the game birds and animals.

Stress factors: Gundog, Herding, Pastoral, and Utility breeds

Because these dogs were bred to be active, lively, persistent and energetic, they will become stressed if they do not have sufficient and appropriate outlets for their desire to move and do. Wonderful sports, competitions and doggy games are now available for owners to enjoy with their working breeds, so there is no excuse for a person to buy one of these dogs and then complain that the dog is tearing up the house, or jumping on visitors or generally barking out of frustration or suppressed energy.

In the UK, the Working Trials, Stock Herding Competitions, Obedience Trials, Agility Competitions, Schutzhund and Ring Sport trials, Retrieving and Hunt, Point Retrieve Trials, Gundog scurries, as well as Search and Rescue dog clubs, are an excellent way to develop the relationship between your dog and you. Dancing With Dogs is especially suitable for athletic, agile and high-energy pastoral breeds like Collies and Shepherds, but if you identify your breed's particular characteristic, and you work out your music and dance routine to suit, most of the breeds in these groups could potentially enjoy this activity.

If we look at some of the other breeds, such as the Terriers, we will see that, because they were selected to hunt

Labradoodle 'Noodle' – the Snownoodle

and kill vermin and other animals that can retaliate when attacked, the most suitable animals were intense, highly reactive to the sight, sound or smell of small prey animals, and indifferent to pain or other influences (such as an owner) when hunting or chasing.

Stress factors: Terriers and Hunting dogs

Such breeds are easily frustrated, easily aroused to action or reaction, and difficult to influence when in that state. Since the breeds range in size from the pocket-sized Yorkshire Terrier, Tenterfield Terrier, and the Czesky Rat Terrier, up to the Russian Black Terrier (which stands taller than a Rottweiler), there are many options to choose from to suit your lifestyle. If you expect them to lie about like house rugs, and only come alive when the family is home at the weekend, you will be extremely sorry and will regret your mistake! These dogs are all bred to hunt and chase; many were developed to dig frantically and energetically for hours, and quite a few were developed to fight other dogs.

Many Terriers that are stressed because they are cooped up all day, will direct their stress outwards in the form of barking, showing aggression towards dogs and animals, and destructive behaviour, or inwards in stereotypical behaviours such as chewing and licking sores, pacing, circling or shadow chasing.

Mastiff puppy

Terrier-racing is a sport that is open to all smaller Terriers, whilst the larger Terriers (Airedales, Russian Blacks etc) can excel at the Working Trials and Agility competitions. The trick with getting Terriers to work for you rather than just chasing the things that interest them, is to prevent them from chasing anything other than your toys. But your toys must be the most exciting, and noisy of all, and preferably should involve squeaking, tugging and chasing. So a squeaky ball on a long rope is ideal.

Every time your Terrier wants to chase something else, you prevent it (extending leads and long lines are ideal in this situation), and then swing your special tuggy around excitedly. Your dog will quickly learn to look at you as soon as a potential prey item is spotted, and you will equally quickly whip out a special toy and have an exciting game of tuggy, so that the frustration of not being able to chase the prey in the distance, is released onto the 'prey' in your hand. Handy tip – always have a back-up toy which is even squeakier or noisier, so that when your dog gets hold of the original, you can wave your new 'better' one around, and the original will be spat out in the hope of getting hold of the new one.

Bull Breeds, and Mastiffs or Molosser Breeds

These breeds range from the French Bulldog to the Great Dane and the Preso Canario and these dogs possess a mixture of some of the tendencies of the Terriers (the indifference to pain when aroused, the determination and tenacity to get hold of the prey animal – even if that is another dog), with some of the cooperative ability of the Working breeds. The Mastiff or Molosser types were dogs that were often used to guard properties (Bullmastiff, English Mastiff), or livestock (Anatolian Shepherd Dog, Kuvasz, Sarplaninac) or to hunt larger prey such as Boar, or Wolves (Great Dane, Cane Corso), and needed to be relatively calm and manageable, but determined and strong. Many were bred for fighting other animals or each other, so they are relatively peaceably towards people, but need to be trained very early in life to develop impulse-control around other animals.

And this is why an American Pit Bull Terrier can become an excellent Pet Assisted Therapy Dog, despite the breed's formidable reputation as a killer. If the Pit Bull also shares the Mastiff characteristics of being slow to react and quick to calm down, this combination of lack of reaction if accidentally hurt (if a child or someone in a nursing home stands on a foot, or pinches an ear), and a desire to be with people, is a chief requirement for Therapy work.

Stress factors – Bull Breeds, and Mastiffs or Molosser Breeds

Teaching any of the fighting breeds to play and then calm down on cue, is essential from the age of about four weeks. These big, strong dogs are sensitive – they require exercise in short bursts, and the companionship of people. They need to be rewarded for showing Calming Signals (see Appendix) to other animals, and the recall to a hand target, with sit and wait is a basic exercise that must be taught as soon as the puppy arrives home. These dogs will be stressed if they are not taught ways to cope with the attentions of other dogs or animals. They may become unpredictable in their responses, and may show aggression or a 'bullying' attitude. Those that combine Terrier and Mastiff characteristics, such as the Boerbull, need to be given an outlet for their intelligence and desire to work. Schutzhund, Ring Sport, Search and Rescue, and Stock Dog Trials (more familiar to US and Australian dog trainers) are all ideal ways for these breeds to expend energy, use their brains, and develop a close rapport with their humans.

Hounds – Sight, Smell and Speed

The Hound Group includes the bendiest legs, as well as the speediest chasers, and the sniffiest noses of all the breeds. Beagles, Pocket Beagles, Dachshunds, and Bassetts are Hounds, as well as Borzois (bred to chase down wolves), Greyhounds, Afghan Hounds and Sloughies (rabbit and hare dogs), and of course the St Hubert's Hound, better known as the Bloodhound (famous for hunting down people). The type of Hound is categorised by the way the dog hunts – using its nose primarily, or its sight (these are also referred to as Gazehounds). Whether the hunting drive is triggered by the sight of something moving, or by the smell of something hidden, the fact is that all these dogs were bred to chase down and corner their prey. It is what they love to do and what they would prefer to do, if given a choice.

Stress factor – Hunting Hounds

These dogs need to feel the wind in their ears and a scent in the nose. However, they are also sensitive and

Above: Czech wolfdog

Below: Wirehaired pointer

Above: Saxon

gentle in the home, and dogs like retired Greyhounds can be wonderful companions. Because they are so tactile, and love being stroked and touched, many members of the Hound Group excel as family dogs. But they must be given an outlet for this desire to hunt and chase, or their frustration can turn into self-mutilation, constant attention-seeking, or depression. Lure-coursing is a sport that many hunting hounds, large or small, absolutely love. The chance to freely chase a twisting, turning, fleeing 'prey' allows them to release this in-built desire, and enables them to relax and lounge around the home for the rest of the week. Smaller hunting hounds like the Dachshund, can enjoy the 'Earth Dog Trials' (where they have to dig out the 'prey'), whilst all hounds will enjoy being taught how to track and trail for fun.

Below: Hector

'Toys R Us' – Toy and Miniature breeds

Although there are tiny Terriers, they may not be part of the Toy Group. This group is a collection of dogs that were mainly bred to be companions for people, either as decorations and ornaments, or as little house dogs, plus there are an increasing number of miniature versions of larger working breeds and Terriers. Miniature Bull Terriers, Teacup Poodles, English Toy Spaniels, and Toy Fox Terriers are now available alongside the more familiar Chihuahas, and Toy Poodles.

Many of these little dogs make delightful companions and fun dogs to own – particularly breeds like the

Affenpinscher, and the Papillon. They can be exercised relatively easily, and usually enjoy human company. Unfortunately, miniaturisation brings the health problems that they may inherit, which can be potentially crippling – especially the slipping patella (or kneecap) that causes so many small breeds to hop or skip whilst walking. People find this hopping action cute, but it actually tells us that the dog is in pain, which many owners are unaware of this. Also, many small breeds suffer from chronic mouth, teeth and gum problems which are treated with great difficulty by vets.

Stress factors for 'Toys R Us'

How can such dear little doggies ever be stressed, in a loving home? Well, the fact is that, small dogs are big dogs that are scaled down, and they need exercise, brain food, and respect for their canine social needs. 'Yorkshire Terrorists' as they are called, are tiny Yorkshire Terriers that are carried about in the arms of their doting owners. Why terrorists? Because they look so cute, and then they growl, snap at and bite any people who come up to pet the sweet little puppy. Small Dog Syndrome is very real.

People buy little dogs because they want them to be animated toys. Rather than teach them how to interact appropriately with dogs and people, they carry them around – these days in various handbag-style carriers. The dogs are frustrated, anxious about dealing with other dogs because they don't understand 'Dog Talk', frightened because they feel trapped up high and constantly being approached by strangers, with no escape route. As the stress level rises, and the dog has no way of dealing with it, the dog becomes more and more reactive, and triggers more and more quickly. The small dog becomes a ferocious little savage. The owner cannot trust the dog to interact appropriately with people or other dogs, so the dear little cute little darling becomes a virtual recluse.

Small dogs need to go to puppy class, learn how to interact nicely and safely with other dogs, children and people, and get plenty of healthy off- and on-lead exercise. It is fine to carry them around, but they also need to learn what other dogs learn, so they can 'talk Dog', and the owners should learn to 'Talk Dog' also. And they need to learn how to play. Many cat toys (motorised ones particularly) are great for small dogs to play with in the house.

Smartest dogs in the world

So many people want to believe that they have an incredibly clever dog or breed. Many writers claim that the Border Collie is the most intelligent, whilst I personally know for a fact that my own Rottweilers were far and away the smartest dogs in the world!

However, the sober fact is that even very clever dogs die eventually, and will be unlikely to transmit that cleverness to new generations. Intelligent dogs escape from kennels, houses and yards, and cannot be kept contained quietly for days on end – they need stimulation, and engrossing activities. (*Red* – the Lurcher, at Battersea Dogs and Cats Home in London, made the headlines when he regularly let himself and all his friends out of their kennels at night and then raided the bins and played till morning.) In short, they don't make ideal pets, nor do they enjoy routine. Obedience to commands and intelligent thinking are opposite qualities that only sit together in moderation. A really clever dog does not want to herd sheep all day – but will find another way to amuse itself. Intelligent dogs solve problems, and try to initiate things, rather than await orders.

You can say any foolish thing to a dog – and the dog will give you a look that says: 'Wow, you're right! I never would've thought of that!'

—Dave Barry

Left: Choccies are OK!

2006

Chapter TEN

Foundation Training

You have socialised your puppy; you have introduced it to principles of learning and started the habit of learning which will help it for the rest of its life. But now you want to be able to walk down the street on a loose lead with your puppy, and continue this, even if the puppy grows up to be big, strong, impulsive and lively.

Well here is a step-by-step way to introduce your puppy to stay in step with you. We don't use any formal commands. This exercise simply mean: 'Walk with me as I stroll'. Crufts obedience it isn't, but cheerful relaxed exercise with your dog, most certainly.

'Before people used to stare at me because I was different, now they stare at me because I am special, with Ben at my side.'

—Wendy H & Ben

Action Cue: 'Let's go'

The cue for this action is the words *'Let's go'*. The aim of the training is to encourage the dog to understand where the 'Let's go' position is (on the left side of the person with the dog's head slightly in front of the handler's knee and the body parallel to the handler in the direction of travel), and then to try to take up that position whenever the handler says: 'Let's go'. This is not the obedience exercise called 'heel'. That comes later.

Short and sweet

All sessions should be no more than 3–5 minutes in length. Use an egg timer if you have problems remembering to stop, or set an alarm. Stop after the length of time, regardless of whether the dog is doing it well or is confused. Dogs also learn by relaxing and thinking about the lesson, so you must stop before the dog becomes tired or tense.

Reinforce where you want the dog to be

If you want a dog to recognise a particular position, the dog needs to get reinforced/rewarded/treated/played with in that position. Therefore, before you start training, you need to have a treat bag and toys ready on your RIGHT side, away from the dog. Once you start

Left: Eurasier puppy learns to 'let's go'

This page and opposite: Outdoor puppy classes

training, you ALWAYS treat the dog from the left, with your left hand, and only in the position where the dog's head should be. If the dog's head is not there, keep your hand, with the treat inside a fist, hanging in the correct position and the dog will quickly change position to be able to receive the treat from your fist – which will open at the correct moment. This stage only lasts for a couple of sessions, and then you need to move on to Treat Transfers and Intermittent Reinforcement.

Treat transfers

Your left hand is always empty when the dog checks, but when you want to reward the dog, you TRANSFER a treat from the right side to your left hand which is waiting in the right position. Your right hand goes across your body or behind your body to your left. Don't move your left hand across to try to get the treat from the bag, or your right hand.

Every time you move your left hand away from that position, the dog will follow it out of the 'Let's go' position, so your aim is to keep the left hand down near where you want the dog's head to be.

Start at the end

The aim of the session is for the dog to take up the position beside you. So that is where you start the session. You don't start walking and hope the dog will guess what you want. Simply put the dog on lead (preferably on a Working Wonders Belt, www.ninabondarenko.com) stand still, and hold your left hand with the treat in a fist, down where you want the dog's head to be. The moment that the dog is facing forwards in the same direction as you, and is nosing, sniffing, touching, looking at your hand, say 'X' and open your hand. If the dog is quick, it will catch the treat, but try to be sure the dog gets that first treat by dropping it as the dog is watching.

Repeat this a few times until the dog is starting to anticipate that your hand will have a treat and the treat appears as soon as the dog takes up the correct position.

The dog should now have an understanding that the best position to be in is beside you and looking up at you.

You will now change the criteria for the dog. This explains to the dog that the 'Let's go' position may move, and the dog must follow it to find the reinforcement.

One small step

Now it is time to change the criteria. Take one step to the left and reinforce. This may surprise the puppy, so be quick to have your hand with a treat ready, to reassure the puppy that life is still good, and staying beside the leg is a good idea.

Reinforce a couple of times, then take another small step to the left. Because you are going to the left, your dog will move out of your way, in order to stay near where the treats come from. Do not pull your hand away, because this will pull the puppy out of position. The more the puppy practises the right position, the more it becomes automatic for the puppy to just move straight there as soon you move.

This is such a simple thing to do when a puppy is small – they learn it so quickly, and it becomes a habit that should be a habit of a lifetime. And it is all based on motivating the puppy to do the right thing without question, yet without force. It only takes a few sessions of five minutes each day, but it gently builds the relationship with your dog based upon mutual cooperation.

Endal was trained using motivational techniques from the age of seven weeks. He won the PDSA Medal for his emergency response to Allen's accident, when he got a blanket from under the wheelchair seat, got Allen's mobile phone and held it for him, and lay next to him to keep Allen warm. He then went and barked at the hotel door to get help.

Most puppies can also learn new things in this way, and if they start early, they love to experiment. A new owner can teach one of the many wonderful skills Endal knows, by following a step-by-step sequence. In this way, puppies can graduate top of the class.

By teaching component behaviours, and then allowing the puppy to experiment with those behaviours, we can develop the ability not only to learn and problem solve, but also the ability of the puppy to deal comfortably with stress and conflict.

Difference between lure, bribe and reward

A lure is when you hold food virtually on the pup's nose to achieve a change in position; for example to teach a baby pup to sit or down. You can then use a target stick for the puppy to follow with its nose, in return for a reward.

A bribe is when you have a pocket or bag of tasty treats that the dog keeps trying to get off you. The dog learns nothing from this.

A reward is delayed slightly – for example you have treats on the worktop and you have to go over and get them to reward the behaviour. This reinforces the idea that good things don't always come immediately. But the puppy thinks that it's worth pleasing you, because, even if you don't seem to have food on you, the puppy is likely to get a reward. So the puppy doesn't look for treats, but just offers the behaviour and waits for a reward.

Right: Bella learns submission to cope with older dogs

Homing signals
Verbal tone training

"Ek, Ek, Ek, EXCELLENT!"
or
"EK marks the spot"

Spot needs information when he tries to learn something. There are various ways we can give that information and some are more effective and easier for a dog to receive than others.

Homing signals are rather like a Warmer–Colder Training Game for dogs. We use our voice to play the warmer–colder game, and the trainee knows when they are getting close to the target because the trainer's voice is getting excited. Homing pigeons follow the signal to get home, and, in the same way, the Homing signal is like verbal landing lights for dogs.

In order to guide a dog to reinforcement in order to get a reward, the dog needs information. Humans are verbal and tend to use their voice. Dogs are non-verbal and tend to use their eyes and ears to work things out. Indeed we can say as a general rule:

- Humans: voice and hands
- Dogs: ears and eyes and nose

So if a dog is going to learn something, it needs information from humans, preferably about whether what the dog is doing is likely to earn reinforcement. This information needs to be delivered in a way that dogs understand easily, regardless of whether the human is an experienced trainer or not.

Enter 'the homing signal'

What do metal detectors, a pilot's audio warning, the warmer–cooler game, and Ian Dunbar's auto-shaping box have in common? Answer: they use an audio cue, rising in tone and increasing in frequency to indicate how close to a target you are. The tone falls or stops the further away you get from a target. If the target is something you want (metal in the sand, levels of radioactivity, correct altitude level, or a dispensed treat), you modify your action to make the sound rise and speed up, until it reaches the target. This is

Above: Put that in your pipe! Confidence building

marked by the *End Sound* and you are rewarded. This was in effect, what I was doing with the 'yes, yes, YES, YES!!!' of my earlier training efforts. However, I needed another piece to complete the behavioural training puzzle. Then I met Stephanie London who introduced me to the work she had been using with her dogs. Stephanie showed me how she taught her rescued Cavalier King Charles dog 'Cricket' to use the word-sound 'X' to target where she indicated.

By adding my rising and speeding up tone, to the use of a non-word as the tone-link and adding 'Excellent!' as the end marker to tell the dog that a reinforcement was now due and payable, I have been able to teach volunteers at Canine Partners, as well as experienced and novice trainers in many different countries, how to improve the way they give training information to their dogs. More importantly, I was able to give an effective technique to the disabled applicants who were learning how to work with a Canine Partner Assistance Dog.

Since many of these people cannot click, or cannot control their limbs sufficiently for good timing, the Homing Signal is a wonderful and effective training tool.

You read about Canine Partner *Orca* winning a PDSA Medal in Chapter 2. It was Cheryl's use of Homing Signals that helped him to help her. If you remember, Orca was trained in Canine Partner's basic emergency procedures. This means that he should get the phone and then lie down beside the person (Partner) to keep them warm until help arrives.

Orca repeatedly tried to do this, but Cheryl needed him to go away and bring someone to help her. A clicker would have been useless because her hands were trapped, but she had her voice.

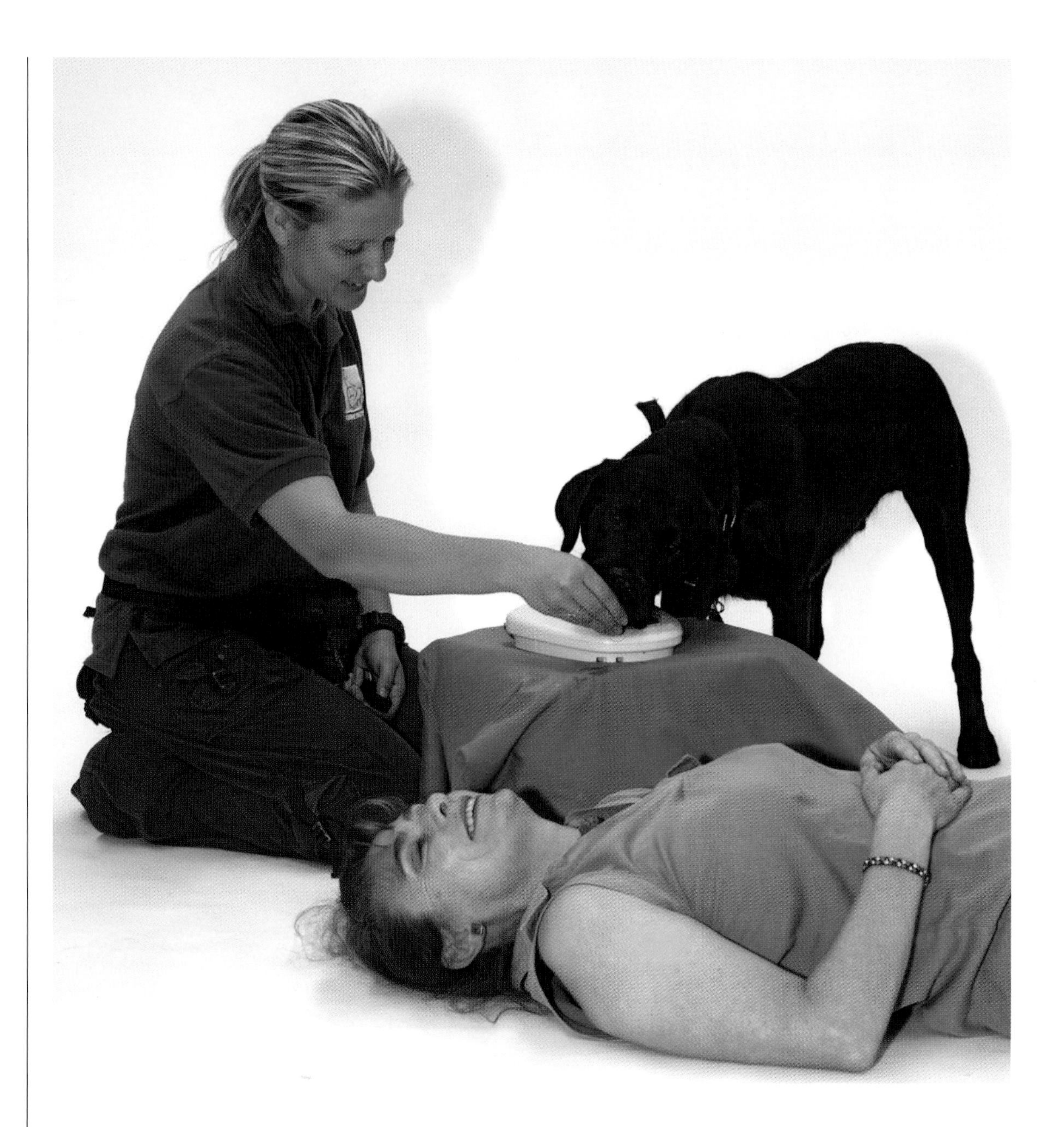

Rewarded near fallen person

By giving him a command (even one that he didn't know: 'go and get help') and then using the Homing Signal as Orca turned away from her, Cheryl was able to convey the following information to Orca:

- Even though you have been trained to come down here to help me – Don't!
- Move away from me and keep going
- Do something else that involves bringing something ('get')
- The situation is urgent and different from normal (even though the 'normal' is only a couple of months of routine together).

By following the Homing Signal that reinforced him to move away, out of sight, Orca was able to use his problem-solving skills, to try different behaviours in this situation.

His first attempt to 'get help' caused him to run up to a man who was exercising his dog on the sports field.

Learning to help the human partner out of bed

Seeing the dog running loose, the man attempted to put the dog in his car to take him to a rescue centre. Orca, like all Canine Partners is trained to go quietly when his collar is taken by strangers. This is an emergency procedure, to ensure that hospital or emergency staff can safely take care of the dog should something prevent the Canine Partner from commanding or controlling their dog. In this instance, Orca (against his training) resisted being taken to the car, slipped his collar and ran back to Cheryl, who was drifting in and out of consciousness. Again she used a Homing Signal to 'get help' and send him away from her.

This time he ran until he found a jogger, running the opposite way from Cheryl. The dog jumped up and down in front of the jogger, impeding his forward movement – then ran a few steps towards where Cheryl lay in the ditch. He then waited for the jogger, then ran back to him. After Orca had repeated this sequence several times, the jogger decided to follow the dog – and was led to the ditch in which Cheryl lay, trapped under her 300lb powered wheelchair. He called the Fire Brigade and Ambulance and Cheryl was rescued.

This is a dramatic, yet practical example of how effective a Homing Signal can be in an emergency. But less exciting, life or death, ways to use a Homing Signal range from teaching walking in a heel position on a loose lead, to teaching a dog to carry an object and place it in your hand/on a surface/in a particular spot, or for an increasing duration of time.

Once a dog recognises that the increasing tone and speed of the 'Ek, Ek' indicates increasing proximity with an opportunity for either reinforcement or completion of an action, the Homing Signal can be used for almost any training exercise.

To introduce the Homing Signal, just use a 'target'.

For example, hold out two fingers together pointing towards the ground. Move very close to the puppy or dog so that the fingers are obvious (right in front of the nose and eyes) and be ready to start saying the Homing Signal 'Ek Ek Ek Ek Ek Ek Ek Ek' as soon as the puppy or dog looks at your 'target' fingers.

Stop saying the Homing signal 'Ek Ek Ek Ek' if the puppy looks away. Restart as soon as it looks back.

As the puppy approaches the fingers to touch them, let the voice get higher and the 'Eks' faster. As

This page
Above: Tugging into up position
Below : Taking the hat off

Opposite page:
Top left: Tolstoi smooth Collie in training
Bottom left: Kermit closing the door
Bottom right: Now to get the clothes out!

soon as the nose touches the target, call out 'Excellent' (terminal bridge) really loudly and excitedly and immediately reward the puppy with a really excellent treat – such as liver cake, or freshly roast chicken, or even something off your own dinner plate.

This is a number 5 treat, meaning that it is top of the range in deliciousness. The puppy should be surprised and excited to get such food for simply touching your outstretched fingers.

The next step is to slightly increase the distance that the dog has to travel to hit the target. This allows you to introduce the *Homing Signal* as a means of letting the puppy or dog know whether they are offering the behaviour that will be reinforced or not. By holding the finger target slightly away from the nose, the puppy must stretch forward. This action will be reinforced by the *Intermediate bridge* sound 'Ek Ek Ek Ek Ek' but it becomes a *Homing Signal*, because the voice starts to rise and the frequency increases as the nose almost touches the target. Again the nose touch is marked 'Excellent!' and then reinforced. The next time hold the finger target slightly further away from the nose, so the puppy must stretch forward, or even take a step or two.

Repeat this exercise several times and then rest. Allow the puppy or dog time to reflect upon what occurred in a calm state (this is called *Latent Learning*). Then start a new session, this time in a different location (perhaps another side of the room), and offer the finger target very close to the nose for the first trial. Use the 'Ek!' (Homing signal) and reinforce the touch. On the next trial, move beside the puppy, so that the puppy must turn its head to see the target, all the time you are using the *Homing Signal*.

'D-Days'

For every increase in difficulty (by changing Direction, Duration, Distraction or Distance), the reinforcement must go back up to a 'level 5'. For repetitions of the same level of difficulty, a lower reinforcement level can be used, and after the third training session, intermittent reinforcement can be used occasionally, to introduce slight frustration and maintain the dog's or puppy's interest.

As soon as the puppy or dog moves directly towards the target, the cue word can be added before the end word (Excellent!). For example – 'touch', ek ek ek or 'target' ek ek ek , or 'here' ek ek ek. The moment the puppy's nose touches the target (your fingers, the switch, the target stick etc), you say 'Excellent!' in a really excited voice and feed the reward. This tells the puppy to aim for the target and then persist until it reaches the target, in order to earn the reward.

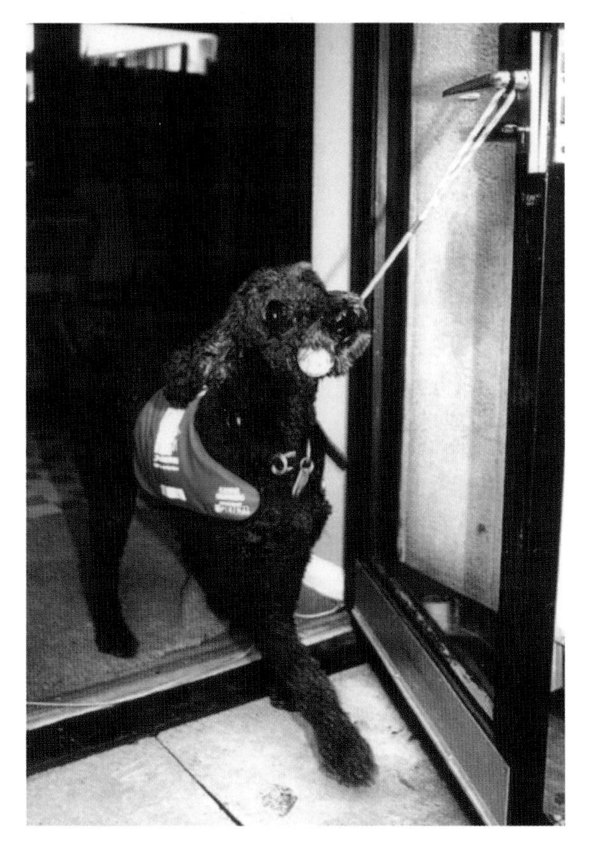

All together now

Once a puppy or dog is comfortable with *Homing Signals*, you can begin to integrate the named actions. This means that the puppy can, for example, learn 'chin, touch my knee', which means that the puppy must put the chin onto the knee. Cup your hand under the puppy's chin and as soon as the puppy rests its head on your hand, you say 'chin, Ek', treat. Once the puppy does that a few times, you move your hand an inch so that it rests on your knee and say 'chin, touch my knee, ek ek ek' as the puppy tries to rest the chin onto your knee. Slip your hand out of the way so that the puppy's chin rests on your knee and say 'Excellent' and a number 5 treat is the reward.

This is a useful skill for any dog – because the dog appears calm, under control and gentle to the general public – and it is an essential command for any dog working in Pet Assisted Therapy, or assistance dog work.

A puppy can also learn to 'take the toy to Bob', or 'put the toys in the basket' if you name the item ('basket' ek, food treat) when the puppy is looking at or sniffing a basket, or 'toys' ek, food treat), whilst the puppy is sniffing or taking hold of a toy.

I guarantee this really works, with a little patience and perseverance – and at the end you will have a dog that is really 'rewarding' for you and which will amaze your friends!

Ever consider what our dogs must think of us? I mean, here we come back from a grocery store with the most amazing haul – chicken, pork, half a cow. They must think we're the greatest hunters on earth!

—Anne Tyler

Chapter ELEVEN

My Partner and I

I've got my life back!

You've given me my life back,
No curfew anymore,
I feel like an adult again,
Nights without carers at my door.

You should have heard the silence,
At the other end of the phone,
When I told the Social Services,
The dog gives my night 'care at home'.

And my little boy can live once more,
Like a seven year old should be,
No longer, feeling too much worry,
He knows Indi's watching over me.

What did I ever do without him?
This golden furry bundle,
This giver of precious life,
That trots by me, as I trundle.

No longer scared to go in shops,
In case there's no one to assist,
No one to take my purse over,
Or pick up the oft-dropped list.

No longer feeling isolated,
Wondering if life will pass me by,
For my life now reflects,
The twinkling in Indi's eye.

When I first became disabled,
I thought my life was gone,
But with my faith, friends, job and Indi,
My life it now goes on!

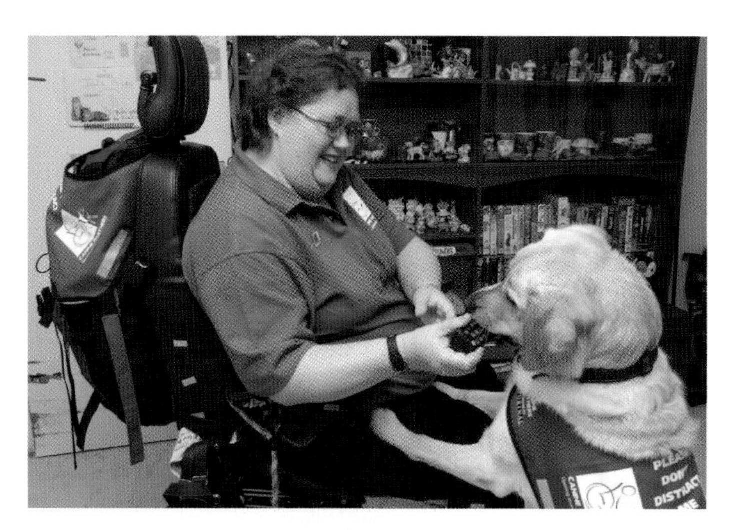

Wendy Ireland and Indi

Diana and Ilya

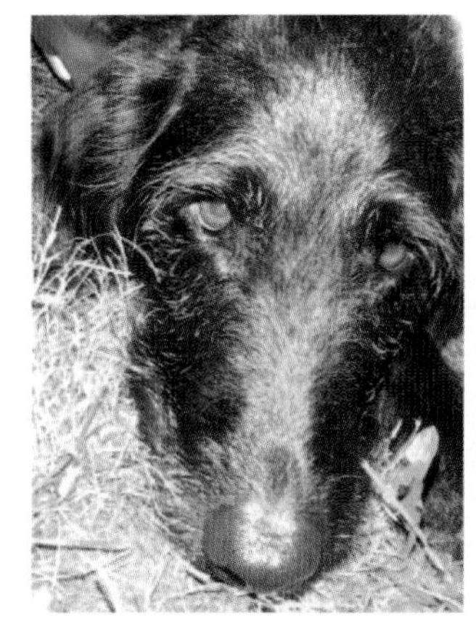

'Every time I see Mum and Ilya together, I marvel at their amazing relationship. Every time I see Ilya close the gate, take the washing out of the machine, automatically pick up something mum dropped, open a cupboard and much more, I always feel amazing inside.

Since Mum and Ilya have been together, I have noticed Mum's confidence grow. The pair have made so many new friends, human and canine, and many new interests.'

Kate Singleton, daughter

'Thank you so much for my superb companion, staunch friend, confidante, helpmate, counsellor, sounding board, comfort cushion, voice trainer and general all round good egg!

He is just a total whizz at agility and is so brave and bold about everything; he just loves every minute. It's such a thrill for me because I was previously very athletic and now watching Ilya do it, it's almost like experiencing a bit of action myself again.'

Diana Singleton, Mother

Maureen George with Kimba

'I had not had Kimba long, but long enough for him to become attached, on their various meetings to a beautiful, female, cream-coloured retriever. Cathy and Heathcliffe had nothing on these two. However, one exceptionally wet day she lured him into a muddy brook, myself devastated on the bank-side. Eventually tail between his legs, head down he rejoined me. Needless to say he experienced earache all the way home: You are a very naughty BOY! Wait 'til you get home! It's the bath for you and no mistake! And so on.... When we arrived home he opened the door and quickly, seeming to forget all other usual tasks, he sped through the lounge. Although drenched but bemused, I followed and found him sitting in the bath, looking very pleased with himself.

Another time, during the summer I cleaned his bark (toilet) area thoroughly on the patio area and left it to dry whilst we went out for the day. We stayed rather late and it was becoming quite dark when I remembered the task. I do have a security light opposite the bark area, but as this only remains on for a short period, I anticipated struggling mostly in the dark. Kimba thought differently. He kept coming out of the lounge and, seemingly deliberately, passing in front of the security light until my task was complete.

Sometimes when training he looks quite pert and will bring items I have not requested. Told 'no', the only word spoken, he drops the article with a sigh and returns with something else. This is usually repeated about 3 to 4 times then suddenly the requested item is brought and then very quickly without instruction and lots of wagging tail and bottom, he returns the wrong ones to their original repository.

There are many other tasks when Kimba teases me, such as taking the daily rubbish to the porch door ready to be taking outside. He knows precisely where it needs to go, but often places it just inside the lounge, then looks for acknowledgement before moving it, a few inches at a time, all the while furiously wagging his tail, to the required place!

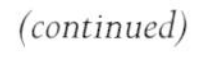
(continued)

Top: Elizabeth Potts & Wesley
Middle: Ian & Ivory (his third dog)
Left: Jake & Spiro (collecting the post)

Sundays, we attend morning church-service. Kimba on the whole is very circumspect, but very much part of it all. Once a month he joins in with fun and games at the family services. Occasionally we have visiting Ministers, who tend to talk for rather a long time. Kimba voices his opinion with a loud 'hmmmm-mmmm…'. Sometimes during long prayers, and at meetings too, Kimba expresses himself during the pauses with heavy breathing. Everyone ends up laughing and no one is offended.

Kimba has also been in the Christmas performances in the last two years. He was Shep, the Shepherds' dog in our Nativity play. When the Shepherds went off to seek Jesus, Kimba quietly stayed with the little ones dressed as lambs. Then, when they moved off, he remained with the stuffed sheep. Last year Kimba was in involved in two performances. During the first, 'Christmas Past' (a mime), Kimba quietly walked up to the stage then sat in the centre with the children. During the second, 'Christmas Present', Kimba took the part of an Alsatian Guard dog. He brought everyone to laughter by laying his head over the side of the stage to sound effects of fierce barking. Later, when the curtain rose for the birth of a child, it was mistakenly dropped again on Kimba. Being the trooper he is, he shrugged it off whilst the cast danced the Can-Can over him and sang 'Congratulations'. He smiled at the audience before nonchalantly resuming his position.

Kimba rehearsed with the rest of the cast and, being writer/director, I took no part in the performances, other than introductions. Needless to say, I was so proud of him.

Kimba enjoys playing his games and is very much a ladies' man. When not looking directly appealing, he will sometimes drop whatever he is carrying whilst shopping, so the ladies run up to help. He then proceeds to pick up the item and wag his tail. He is such a flirt!

When exercising on the cycle paths in our local park areas, I allow Kimba to go ahead, in the knowledge that he does stop for people or cyclists, when required. Often we play Hide & Seek, a favourite for both of us, but I am unable to do this too frequently because he stops at every little cut-off, in case I try to sneak off and hide!

I truly believe Kimba is part human too, because he is so tuned in. One day I was in the park with Kimba and my carer when she informed me she was leaving the job. I was quite upset and, trying to take the edge off the situation, I said: 'I wish I'd brought Kimba's ball or kong to throw for him'. Kimba at this point rose, walked three trees down, and came back with a stick. He KNEW I needed distraction.

Earlier this year, a northern friend was visiting. In an attempt to help, she offered to get the washing from the machine. Kimba, resting in the lounge, rushed through to the kitchen and proceeded to open the washing-machine door and take the washing out. Competition is a wonderful thing!

Another day my friend had kindly hoovered for me, whilst Kimba and I were out. In doing so she had moved my manual chair out of the normal position for Kimba to bring for me to transfer into. Undeterred, he worked out how to manoeuvre the chair completely round into the right position, then proceeded to bring it to me.

Apart from being a ladies man, Kimba is quite a celebrity in this area. Chemists, banks, doctors, nurses, dentists and shopkeepers all vie for his attention. One of my friends is a police driving instructor and frequently brings officers round to meet him. He has even been known to stop whilst driving, in order for the student officers to meet Kimba. Ah, fame!

On regular visits to the doctors/dentists (same building) Kimba reaches up to the exceptionally high counter, to say 'Hello', inform them we are there, collect prescriptions, etc. each time with his appealing look. Even if we don't have a need to visit, he still likes to go there, to say 'Hello'.

I could go on indefinitely, Nina, for being partnered with Kimba brings me a great deal of love, comfort, happiness, laughter and the strength to reach down within myself, to face each day the challenges and adventures that life offers.'

The Fencott family

My story: Sarah Fencott

'I've always wanted a dog, ever since I was little, but my parents always said 'no', but fate led us to a bright purple bunch of people, at a country park and there we found out about Canine Partners. I was only 13 at the time, so I was too young to have a full partnership, so as a family we started to foster dogs for the odd week, here and there.

We had lots of dogs and puppies come to stay with us, but they always had to go back to wherever they came from after the holiday was up. But then a fluffy nervous dog came to stay for a while called Danny. He was three and had been partnered with someone else before, but there had been problems, which I wasn't too sure about, so he came to us for a rest. We bonded immediately and after a few days he started working again. It was so cool, 'cos I had a gorgeous dog that could go everywhere with me. I know the time would come that he would have to go back to his partner, but then I got a letter from Canine Partners saying: "We would like Danny to stay with you, as we think he has bonded with you and we would like him to become your working partner".'

I couldn't believe it, I had a dog and I don't have to give him back. Of course, we celebrated in the pub together … now I love Danny to bits and life really begins.

My story: Danny Fencott

'I wouldn't call it work being a working dog; more like fun being with my mummy all day. I mean, yeah OK it's a partnership, so I still do lots of work for her like helping her around our house taking her to places and helping her do stuff she can't do but then she helps me as well by feeding me, taking my to the park, giving me a nice brush or just cuddling up together watching TV at night. I've been with Sarah for 3½ years (or 5 of your human years) and I still love her to bits I had lots of other mums and dads before I arrived at Sarah's house and I was a bit stressed out and down on everything so I wasn't working but she nursed me back to health and as soon as she got into trouble I put my coat back on and switched back into Danny the working dog. Sure, there's parts of my job I hate like when we go shopping; it's sooooooo boring 'cos she's so indecisive and spends ages looking at clothes but I know that I will be rewarded by a play in the park or a drink and a packet of crisps in the pub.'

Bottom left: Paul Beauchamp & Willow
Bottom right: James & Nemo

Margie and Renee

12 April 2005

It is almost a year since I was introduced to Renee, my Canine Partner. She is a wonderful yellow Labrador. Her birthday is on 17th July. She will be three years old; in her prime so to speak. We have been through a lot this year, learning from each other, getting to know each other – how we think, how we react, how to play and how to rest. We have had our ups and downs, but most of them have been ups.

14 April 2005

As a partnership we have done a lot together, conferences, training, loads of boring meetings. We've travelled on trains, buses and coaches, hundreds of miles by car, one trip to the Isle of Wight by ferry (this was in our first week of partnership). The only thing we haven't tried is going by air, but I'm sure this will come in time. Renee and I have stayed in hotels up and down the country, big and small, grand and humble. Renee is a dog that needs to go to the loo quite often, so we have learnt to take advantage of flowerpots, tree stumps, high advantage points where there might be some grass!

Sometimes around London there are special dog loos – places fenced off in recreational parks where,

Margie and Renee in the sunshine (Margie works for SCOPE and Renee goes everywhere with her)

sometimes, people do pick up after their dog. I will leave it to your imagination when this doesn't happen – some human beings are awful (it really doesn't take much to take a plastic bag with you), but there you are, that is my rant and rave for the day. However, it must be very strange for some people seeing Renee and myself creeping out of the hotel at dawn, to find some vantage place for Renee to have a pee!

20 April 2005

As for my personal care, Renee has done extremely well. From day one she has always taken off my socks, but such is her training that she learns all the time and this has developed now into her helping me off with trousers, jumpers, socks, shoes, retrieving items such as the phone, my glasses – I never know where I put them – so we play hunt the thimble! Taking items from upstairs to downstairs, even managing to select certain items of clothing from my wardrobe and cupboards.

I am in the process of teaching Renee to help me turn back the bed in the morning. She is beginning to show her own initiative: I often catch her looking at me to see what I am going to do next and to anticipate what I might need. I was once considering where I had put my hearing aid and, lo and behold, I looked down and she had it in her mouth.

Renee has developed relationships with the other animals in the house: the pugs, Rosie and baby. She really enjoys going out for a walk together with the pugs. They have often been frightened of other dogs, but now they know they have a big sister this is changed, and they are not frightened at all; in fact they often challenge other dogs.

She is still a bit wary of the cat, Mr Parker. This is because he sometimes dabs her in passing, so if Renee is cornered she is reluctant to go past so mummy has to come and rescue her! But I don't mind that, as I'd rather be safe than sorry. Yesterday she managed to catch one of the mice, which Mr Parker had got bored with and dropped in the kitchen. However at my expression she immediately dropped the poor little creature and off he scurried under the fridge, only to be caught later in the mousetrap – such is fate. Who would be a mouse?

Ann & Noodle

Alan & Troy

Yvonne Le Mone and Kenya

"Dear every Partner to be on the March training course,

I have never met any of you and you don't know me, but what you are about to go through in the next two weeks, we do share.

Right now you are hoping that you will be partnered with the dog you have tried your best not to get attached to and love on all the assessment days. You may be wondering what lays ahead on the course and how you will manage. You may also be wondering if you will graduate. We all felt like that.

You may never remember these words, in the state of emotional stress that you are in right now. But over the next two weeks, however low you feel, however stupid you think you are because you cannot remember simple easy things that previously were so easy, however tired you get, however awful it all may become, remember many of us have survived a Canine Partner's course before you!

Hold onto the fact that at the end the result WILL BE SO WORTH IT. If like me you have had pet dogs before, having a Canine Partner dog is very different. I had no idea how limited my life had become, until I had Kenya. He has given me my freedom back. He is a constant loving companion, full of fun and joy. I love him far more than any other dog I have ever had. Look forward to that yourselves. I will be sending you all good thoughts and feelings. Well done to have got this far. Your life is about to change for ever.

Yvonne

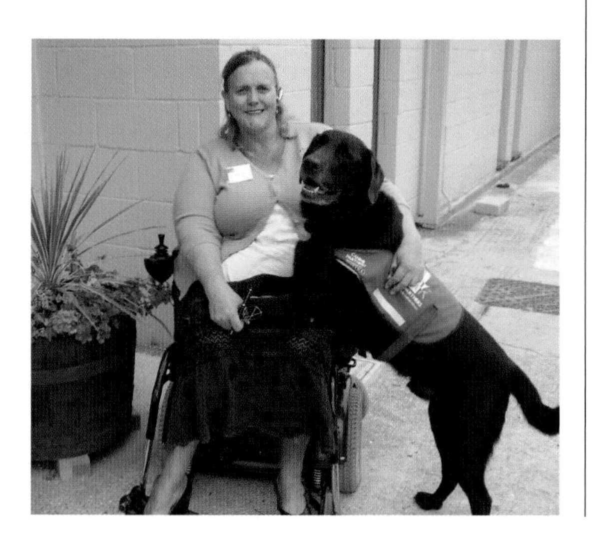

Top right: Judy & Kermit
Bottom left: Jenny & Free
Bottom right: Claire & Ulli

Bernard and Jinx

One Saturday, my wife and I went shopping in Gunwharf Quays in Portsmouth. In a very busy shop, I was beginning to get quite disoriented (I have MS and this sometimes happens in busy, noisy places) so I went to find a quiet corner.

A lady came up to me and said, 'I am sorry to bother you but can my grandson stroke your dog?' 'No problem,' I replied and I moved my wheelchair, plus Jinx towards a young woman accompanied by a child in a buggy. I don't know what was wrong with the child but he sat quite expressionless and motionless in the buggy.

Gran took the child's hand and moved it over Jinx's fur; no reaction. 'Oh, I'm sorry, I thought it would do something for him.' 'Don't worry;' I replied. 'I'll get Jinx to touch him. Go on, Jinx, lick his hands.' Jinx, always wanting to be helpful, dutifully did as he was asked and licked the boy's hand. Again no reaction.

Gran was most upset and so was the boy's mum. 'I'm so very sorry to have bothered you,' she said almost in tears. 'It is no bother. I'd like to try something else, if I may,' I replied. 'Oh please,' said the mum. 'Jinx, give him a kiss; give him a kiss, Jinx; good boy.' I just hoped Jinx would co-operate.

Good old Jinx did just as he was asked, he put his front paws on the side of the buggy and planted a big kiss on the front of the boy's face. Much to everyone's amazement, the boy came out of his trance-like state and laughed and gurgled away quite happily.

I can't begin to explain how I felt. It was so emotional; Gran was crying, Mum was crying, my wife was crying – as were several of a small crowd that had gathered. Us males don't do emotion, do we? Like hell we don't! It chokes me up every time I tell the story; there are tears in my eyes as I'm writing this. How can a little dog perform such a miracle – only the Lord knows.

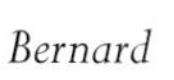

Bernard

Bernard with Jinx

A day in the life of Frodo, the Labrador

I've got a rug on the floor but I hardly ever use it – I like to wake up on the bed next to Steph. It's a comfort thing. She's pretty ropey in the morning to be honest, whereas I'm totally chipper. As soon as the alarm goes off, I roll over and lick her face to wake her. She might say, 'Fro, go and wake James,' which I particularly enjoy. I tug off his quilt and start to lick any bit of bare skin I can find. Drives humans nuts this. You should hear the noise!

Next I get the rubber tug-toy and pull Steph up to a sitting position or, depending how weak she is, she might put her arms round my neck so I can pull her up that way. We have a bit of a chitchat. 'Morning, Frodo. How are you today?' Bit of a cuddle. Then a root about under the bed to find her slippers and the elbow crutches, drag them out with a minimum of slobber and we're away.

Once Steph's up, I follow her everywhere. I tug the bathroom light on and lurk around in case she drops something. All right, so I might have half an eye on the special little nibble she sometimes has secreted about her person to reward the really clever stuff. After all, I'm only canine! But the truth is (just between you and me, mind) she's not completely safe without me. They like to think they're in charge, but we all know who runs things around here. I'm so tuned into her. I can hear a crutch fall across a ploughed field, and in two secs I'll be there to pick it up for her.

It wasn't always like this. Ooh no, no! To begin with, it was dire. A personality clash, you could say. She was 'Frodo do this, Frodo do that' and I'm like: 'Sorry, what did your last slave die of?' We dogs have a life, you know, especially when you're a not unattractive chocolate Labrador in his prime. Washing, it was, mostly. Drove me nuts. She expected me to drag baskets of it out of the machine and into the garden. And she'd freak when it spilt out and got a bit muddy.

Frodo sorts the washing!

Stephanie and Frodo go shopping

Then a mate of mine, another highly trained animal, said to me: 'Look, Frodo. There are humans and humans. There are those who can and those who can't.' Course, we specially trained dogs don't need to bother with those who can – you do what 99% of the canine population do and play dumb … and you get what you want – food, walks, play – by doing zip. Those who can't are our domain. I felt a bit guilty, because I could have been more helpful, but bless her, Steph's a forgiving little thing, and we love each other dearly now.

Steph goes down for breakfast in the stair lift, then I have the tiniest snooze while she has her cup of tea. But I'm on red alert. I can be snoring my brains out, but the minute I hear her move, I'm up. Next it's the washing. I drag it into the basket and through the kitchen door, then I knock the catch off and open the patio door, letting the stupid cat in if she happens to be sitting there.

It's a rare degree of power, this, deciding whether to let that animal in or leave it to mew. Then back inside to find the peg bag. Impressive isn't it?

Once I've helped Steph get dressed, passing her this and that with my mouth, it's off to the shops, not forgetting to collect the keys from the hook in the hall. First the bank – I grab the money from the cash-point and give it to her. Then I take her prescription into the chemist and hand that over. Doing 'Asda' is my favourite.

I gently get everything we need off the shelves, always monitoring the slobber thing. At the checkout, my *pièce de résistance,* handing over the purse. The queue behind is in raptures. I wouldn't be an honest dog if I didn't admit I bask in the glory.

Finally, oh joy, it's off to the park for my walk and if I don't have to pull her electric wheelchair out of the mud – I'm off, like a streak of lighting. A chap has to have some 'me' time. Once we're home, I hang Steph's coat up and put her trainers in the cupboard. Not many people know this, but we trained dogs have our own lavvy. I might be bursting to go, but I've taught myself to wait until I get home, so I can go in my own area in our garden and close the gate behind me. There's nothing quite like your own loo, is there?

Frodo selects some breakfast cereal

If she wants to watch TV, I curl up under Steph's knees so she can rest her feet on my back. Then it's another snooze for me, but it doesn't last long. I bring her the phone when it rings, and I can usually rely on her to gas long enough for me to have one of those nice twitchy, rabbity sort of dreams.

Steph cooks dinner for herself, James and Emma. She puts the plates and cutlery on a trolley and I drag it into the dining room. A bit hit and miss, this I'll grant you. I keep a special eye on Emma, because she needs me too. I don't like to see her struggling.

At night, I stand guard while the carer bathes Steph, then I help her into bed and settle down beside her. She needs me close.

Not many people know this, but dogs pick people, not the other way round. I picked Steph and I consider myself extremely lucky. I won't perform for others. I hate it when humans with all their bits in working order expect me to put on some kind of show. 'Get this, Frodo; do that.' Well, sorry, but I'm not a circus act. I'll have a scratch, a yawn and turn on my 'dumb canine' act. When I'm, off duty, I'm mummy's 'Froddle Woddles' and I want a serious amount of fuss. After all, I am just a dog…"

Opposite page:
Top left: Suzie & Lex
Top right: Eileen & Sailor
Bottom: Steve & Mozart

None of the facts has been changed to protect the authors of these stories!

CANINE
PARTNERS

CANINE
PARTNERS
PURINA

Suggested Further Reading

Understanding and Training Your Puppy – video by Nina Bondarenko – produced for Purina in association with Canine Partners

Understanding Your Dog by Eberhard Trumler – The Trumler Research Centre, Germany

Partners for Life – Jane Bidder, Orion Press, Illustrated by Nina Bondarenko

How Dogs Learn – Burch and Bailey – Allen & Unwin

Owners Guide to Better Behaviour in Dogs – William Campbell

Books by Dr Ian Dunbar – James Kenneth Publishers

Culture Clash – Jean Donaldson – James Kenneth Publishers

Dog and a Dolphin 2.0 – Karen Pryor – Sunshine Books (USA)

Don't shoot the Dog – Karen Pryor – Sunshine Books (USA)

Don't shoot the Dog Study Guide – Sunshine Books (USA) pamphlet

Calming Signals – book and video – Turid Rugaas

Minds of Their Own – Lesley Rogers Allen & Unwin

The Parrot's Lament – Eugene Linden – Souvenir Press

Bridge and Target – www.synalia.com

Gary Wilkes – www.clickandtreat.com

Marion Breland Bailey and Bob Bailey www.hsnp.com/behavior/

Additional Notes

At an international level, new organisations are being established to review and propose policies for the health, mental and social well-being of animals and to draw up guidelines for Human ethics, responsibilities and obligations – organisations such as the International Companion Animal Welfare Conference (ICAWC); International Association of Animal Behaviour Consultants (IAABC); the International Association for Human Animal Interaction Organisation (IAHAIO); the Ethnologists for Ethical Treatment of Animals (EETA), many Animal Welfare lobby groups, World Wildlife protection groups, and finally small organisations dedicated to research and promulgation of these issues, such as Society for Companion Animal Studies (SCAS) – for which I have been a Trustee and Advisor and for which Dr Elizabeth Ormerod MRCVS (a co-founder of Canine Partners) is the current chairman.

'The Jeffery Method of Horse Handling' by Kel B Jeffery describes a wonderful behaviour-based horse management and training system developed in Australia in the 1960s (out of print).

What is a working dog?

The situation in Europe and to a lesser extent America, is very different to that in Australia, where I was born. Dogs are utilised in almost every conceivable field and where such services are no longer required (as in for example the messenger dogs); competitions based on the original task are still held. Some of the many fields in which dogs work include: ambulance dogs, messenger dogs, border-patrol dogs, guide dogs, hearing dogs, therapy dogs, sled-dogs, carting or hauling dogs, disaster-dogs, police, army, navy, air force and related service-dogs, customs-dogs, mine-dogs, tracker and trailing dogs, sheep and cattle dogs (as well as other livestock control, such as geese, turkeys etc); Search & Rescue (SAR) and avalanche dogs; and the sports in which dogs regularly compete include agility, Diensthund (this means 'Service Dog' as accepted in the UK and Australia – a dog working for Customs, or one of the other services), sheep and cow-dog trials, obedience, back-packing, sledding, weight-pulling, high-jump, 'Ring Sports', Schutzhund, tracking and all the hunting,

coursing and field-trials. This is by no means an exhaustive list but gives an idea of the variety of activities that people use dogs for in Europe.

What is motivational or behavioural training?

Scientific research by Scott and Fuller in the 1950s, was the foundation of a modern study of canine behaviour. The later experiments by the Brelands and the Baileys, researching behaviour at the Animal Behaviour Enterprises in the USA for the US military and later for commercial projects, can be seen on the video *Patient Like the Chipmunks* – Version 1: The Story of Animal Behaviour Enterprises. www.hsnp.com/behavior/). This video is amazing – until you have seen the chickens playing Noughts and Crosses, or the cat sitting for an hour in an airport, you really won't believe what is possible with positive training methods.

The modern development of practical Operant Conditioning – a powerful and effective tool for modifying behaviour, utilised by Gary Wilkes and Karen Pryor – has allowed trainers to move away from the theory of dog training based upon coercing the dog into position. The field of practical dog training with a theoretical basis has mushroomed. Dr Ian Dunbar set a precedent when he established the Association of Pet Dog Trainers in the United States as an open-membership organisation designed to encourage trainers to attend conferences and seminars in order to open their minds to new information and thinking about dog behaviour and training, and also about human behaviour. This helped the spread of up-to-date information to pet owners throughout the world.

Affenpinschers